12 BLOCKS

SHORT STORIES FROM THE 60'S

SAM PAGANO

DEDICATION

To Pam, Peter, and Tommy

To whom I would like to
thank for all their love and support
and to my childhood friends
who inspired me to write
this memoir.

TABLE OF CONTENTS

INTRODUCTION

This story is about growing up in East Newark, NJ, and the surrounding small towns in the '50s and '60s. The stories are about having fun in what seemed to my friends and me to be the most fun and simple time in human history. We were not aware of, and therefore, did not care that the Korean War had just ended, the Cold War was going strong, the Cuban Missile Crisis was current, and Viet Nam was about to take over the headlines. All we were on top of was our neighbors' roofs and the latest monster movies. This book is not only about the fun we had and the games we played but also about the love we shared for our little world and for each other.

The stories are an accurate memoir of my childhood, although some names and identifying details have been changed to protect the privacy of individuals.

It's the mid 60's in East Newark NJ, and all Sam Pagano and his buddies want to do is get out of their 12-block town. At the same time, they love every second spent running around in their worldwide playground of East Newark, Harrison, and Kearny. Schooldays spent at St. Anthony's Grammar school. Saturdays at The Warner Theater, Saturday nights at The Arrow Bar and Pizzeria. Youth sports that included lots of roof climbing kick the can, stickball, and cards for comics. Sundays after Mass, the pool room, and pasta. Come join Sam, Frankie, Charlie, Pete, Pepi, Tootsie, Lefty, and the rest of the gang for a stroll back in time.

CHAPTER 1

Let's Get Out of Town

"What we needed was a way to get out of town, and even though I shut my eyes and dreamed of a Rocket Ship escape, I knew damn well we were not going anywhere!"

I suppose that first, you want to know about me and the guys. About growing up in East Newark, a small Jersey ethnic melting pot, a town of first-generation Italians, Irish, Polish, and well just about every other tribe you can imagine. As a kid, I spent a lot of time at "The Arrow" with my friends. It was my father's Tavern and Pizza Parlor, smack in the heart of Harrison - four blocks and a bridge from Newark, a half-block away from Kearny, and only a mighty egg toss away from my East Newark backyard.

One thing I loved about East Newark is how easy it was to get out of East Newark. Well, Technically, it was easy; just walk a few blocks in any direction, from any starting point in town, and "Bam" you were out of town. OK, close your eyes walk ten feet, and now, where are we? *Close your eyes and guess* was a fun game we played while walking from one end of our universe to the other. One way we knew for sure that we wandered out of town was when we would see or stumble upon some grass. Sure, some of us had grass in our backyards, and a few of us even had a tree. The tree in my yard had a great big fun treehouse; well maybe not a house, but it did have a few two by fours to step on, climb up onto a limb, and jump off of into our four by four backyard pool. My best friend Pete's rent-a-garage back yard was even more fun. No grass, nothing but concrete, where we played stickball, basketball, and football. Every game came with a built-in time out when our neighbors came to park cars or get their stuff out of the eight rented garages.

Pete, John, Billy, Charlie, and all the rest of my St. Anthony's fifth-grade friends used to wonder and argue about the number of blocks you would have to walk before you left East Newark and stepped into either Kearny, Harrison or Newark. I mean, it wasn't all that hard to do because, on any day, we would put our toes down in at least three of the four towns. The hard part was figuring out the steps involved.

My very logical best friend, Pete Borghesi, once made it all very clear to me. Pete lived only about a twenty-yard dash from my home in East Newark. He was also a half-court dribble from Harrison, an infield fly from the bridge into Kearny, and a fifty-yard dash to the Annie Bridge into Newark.

"It depends on where you are starting from and where you are headed. It could be 12 blocks to get to Kearny or turn around and walk one foot and get to Harrison."

"Well, thanks for explaining Pete, it's clear to me now."

"OK, Sam, let's suppose that we cross over the Stickle Bridge and walk three feet deep into Newark then turn around. How many feet will we have to walk to get back onto the bridge and head back to East Newark?"

"Come on, Pete, I'm not that stupid. Anyway, you just explained it all to me three feet!"

"Ah, but what if the Bridge just opened, Sammy Boy?"

And that was in a nutshell, why we called my friend Pete Mr. logic.

As far as I could tell, our classmate Billy Heffern who lived on Second St. next to St. Anthony's church and right across from St. Anthony's school, was not interested in getting out of town or walking anywhere. Anywhere except to school and back at least four times a day.

In fact, the only other place Billy ever talked about going was inside a time machine, back to Dodge City, to shoot it up with Matt Dillon or to ancient Greece to draw swords with The Three Hundred Spartans. Or he would reverse course and head back to the future, where he would land on, and explore, *The Angry Red Planet, Planet X, or America in 1984.*

I guess, Billy really thought that what he said over and over was true. *"East Newark,* 1962 is so boring, nothing to do, nowhere to go."

"Really, Billy? You really think that on Friday when we stuck chewing gum in the keyhole of every lock on every front door on Third Street, that was boring?"

"OK, Sammy, it was pretty funny when Mrs. Riley tried to open the door, and the *Bazooka* stuck on her hand and got all over her nose." "But," Billy kept making his point. "But I bet the gum on Mars would have kept liquefying and expanding till her fingers got stuck inside her nose."

"Wow, that would be so cool and freaking gross," I snorted

"I don't know if it would have, so I guess you'll have to ask your Martian friends how quickly gum melts on Mars?"

Even though his daily trip to school took all of ten seconds, Billy would have to sneak in right before attendance just about every other day. And when he was late for morning prayers (missing the first half of the Hail Mary), he would toss his own 40-yard Hail Mary to Sister Mary Anthony, somehow passing the buck to Matt Dillon or *Buffalo Bill* for his tardiness. He could somehow always find a way to turn his half block walk to school into a Wild West Adventure. I guess that's why we sometimes called him Billy, The Kid!

"How many blocks?" Charlie Lombardi, my mischief mate, asked again and again. Charlie lived three blocks away from my house, right down Third St. past Central Avenue in a tiny apartment above the Official Senate Boys pool room. Charlie would basically tell me that it did not matter if it was one block or twelve blocks. "Who gives a shit?" His argument was, "As long as you get us out of town, Sammy boy, just show us the way, where the hell should we go to anyway?"

"Charlie, let's not worry about the details. We can hop on the number 13 bus, board a plane to Disneyland, or that rocket to the moon we keep hearing about, north or southeast or west, I'm on board as long as you're with me."

John Hess, A.K.A. Mr. Smarty Pants lived so far away, way-way over the Kearny Bridge, that we couldn't walk to his house even when we wanted to. It took way too long, and there was always the chance of running into some of the shithead Kearny kids if we did. Most of the Kearny kids we knew went to Queen of Peace School, way up Kearny Avenue almost halfway to North Arlington. It was a rival Catholic school, but I don't think they taught anything about peace on earth or goodwill towards men, cause every time we ran into them, it was WAR!

The best battle we ever had happened two weeks ago after mass, when somehow and as if by God's plan, we all met up under the bridge between Harrison, East Newark, and Kearny. It was a swords drawn (long snapped off tree branches) stick em in the gut fencing battle that ended only when the three Kearny kids surrendered their sticks. It got even better when Charlie's bright idea to take the shoe-laces from their sneaks and tie their legs together had them down on their knees.

"That's stupid. The Kearny kids can just untie the laces and get up, unless duh! You tie their hands and feet together." As always, Pete provided the clarity that me and Charlie lacked. What he did not offer was more shoestrings, so we unlaced our sneaks, tied hands to

11

feet, and left our fellow Roman Catholic brothers under the bridge.

John, Mr. Smarty Pants, knew and sometimes hung out with most of the Kearny kids and lived only a few blocks from Joey Pizza, one of the brothers that we left under the bridge. John must have been thinking I don't think I'll be playing Dodge Ball with those guys anymore because he kept pestering us to, "go back and untie those guys."

"Come on, John, why? They are fine."

"Sammy, they have been tied up under the bridge for almost an hour."

"We'll get them tomorrow."

"Tomorrow! Bullshit Sammy, it's already been over an hour."

"So, what's the hurry? They're not going anywhere."

We finally gave in to John's pestering, ran back to the East Newark bank, climbed over the fence behind the bank, crawled under the bridge, and saw——shoelaces!

That's when the dead frogs, dead pigeons, dead snakes, live worms, and mud balls started raining down on us from atop the bridge.

Obviously, Pete did not tie knots around wrists as well as he knotted his St. A's school tie every morning. Joey Pizza and the K. Kids were now on top of the bridge, tossing down everything that used to be under the bridge. We dodged most of the crap they hurled, even tried chucking some of it back at them. Still, most of it floated right back at us, making it the funniest Dodgeball, well actually *Dodgecrap* game ever.

Once everyone got back on top of the bridge, everybody was laughing. The issues that had us divided seemed to disappear. Almost!

After a few more laughs, we all decided it was lunchtime, and John wandered back to Kearny, back home with Joey Pizza and the rest of the Queen of Peace Kearny kids.

After three o'clock during the school week, John really did not hang out with us. When the whistle blew at the end of our last class, his Dad would pull in front of St. A's, open the door, John would jump in, and we would usually not see or talk to him till he jumped out right before morning prayers the next day. Unless, of course, one of us needed help with our homework, like sometimes when I actually tried to do the math homework. I might need the answer to what is one plus one half divided by three quarters or what is the square root of Pi? Then ring, ring, ring…. "Hello, Mr. Hess, Is John home?"

Most Sundays were not filled with quite so much sword fighting. Usually, after mass, the guys would meet up for Stickball, Three Feet, and A Lead, Kick the Can, Ringolevio, or Dodgeball. We might start out at my house on Third Street, play *Three Feet, and A Lead* in front of my porch, and depending on the direction we were facing, that three-and-a-half-foot journey could bring us darn close to Pete's cement backyard.

At Pete's, we could shoot hoops, play soccer, or stickball and blast a *Spalding* 200 feet, all the way down to the East Newark School playground, then climb over the 10-foot fence and play Dodgeball.

But at mass this Sunday, while kneeling between the Hail Mary and The Lord's Prayer, Billy whispered in my ear, "Want to play Cards for Comics?" I felt like we were practicing for confession and whispered back, "OK, Billy, in your back yard?" After a nod from Billy and Father Joe's dismissal, I made the sign of the cross and invited the gang (everyone but Pete) over to Billy's.

I didn't see Pete at Sunday Mass. I guess he went to 8 o'clock service. So, after stripping off my Sunday suit, I made the half-block trek to his house on Sherman Ave.

"What's up Sammy?"

"Card's for comics game at Billy's. Everyone will be there."

I showed Pete a few Superman's and a dozen Batman's and sighed when he gave me his famous frown. That frown forced me to pull out my ace of spades, the newest edition of *Famous Monsters Magazine,* the one with a smiling, well kind of groaning, Vincent Price on the cover.

Pete, who was now interested yelled at the top of his lungs, "Mom Sammy's here, we're going to Billy's to play cards for comics!" Then, he ran into his room and came out smiling carrying a few Batman and Superman comics, a smile featuring his missing front teeth forcing me to question him as I did daily.

"So, Pete, I guess you really can't catch Bobby's fastball"? I asked as I always did. Even though I doubted Bobby ever threw a pitch to Pete.

Bobby Kreese was a giant 5th grader at St. A's who could throw a bowling ball as far as I could throw a Spalding. Bobby just had no idea where anything he threw was going, forget trying to hit the corner of the strike zone or of Pete's catcher's mitt.

"Sam, will you please stop with Bobby's fastball crap! If you really cared about my choppers, you would find my missing buck teeth, get me some real toothpaste, and paste them back in Ha Ha Ha."

Along with his missing front teeth, Pete had a brand-new deck of cards, and those Superman and Batman comics that I knew damn well would soon be mine. Well, maybe not all of them but more than a few.

"See you later, Mrs. Borghesi," I said as we left the porch. I knew that if Pete's mom had any idea that Frankie and Charlie would be playing that Pete wouldn't be, but I thought what the hell I'm not telling her and, after all, what's the worst that could happen?

Could Pete lose a few comics or if a stickball game started, maybe a few more teeth?

Could I win as many comics as I dreamed of winning? Comics that inspired my dream to be a superhero, to fly out of town, to go back and forth in time, and from this universe to another universe? Comics sure got me out of town if only in my mind. Now let the games begin.

While walking from Pete's porch to Billy's backyard, I looked 100 feet up the block to Kearny Avenue in Kearny, NJ down the block 50 feet to Fourth Street the Main Street in Harrison and straight ahead 20 feet to Third Street my home block in the dead center of East Newark, NJ Our whole universe was right here.

And despite Mrs. Borghesi's repeated warnings to not get lost, I kind of hoped we would. We certainly knew our way home from Billy's and the 13 routes out of our 12 block playground, yet although we often talked about getting out and the fastest ticket out of town, what I did not know was...

(Why, why we wanted to get out?) I guess someday I/we would get that ticket out of town and find out!

On the other hand, on that day, on the way to the cards for comic's games, I thought about all the comics that would soon be mine and realized that I really wasn't in a hurry to find out or to get out!

CHAPTER 2

Cards for Comics

"Deal me in Frankie. I'm not going any-where, and so as long as I'm stuck here with you guys, I might as well cash in, grab every new Superhero comic and fill

up my pockets with everything St. Antho-
ny will allow!"

Halfway down, Sherman Ave, on the way to the after-mass card game, I was starting to get all excited while trying hard to control my excitement. Even though I knew Billy had invited the rest of the gang over, I still wondered whether Charlie would show up on time? If Billy would bring some of his Dad's Playboys and whether Frankie might actually bring anything at all this time. Something? Anything?

In fifth grade, comic books were my primary source of learning. They really helped me concentrate. Sometimes, and especially during math class, I might stick a Superman mag between the pages of my textbook and glance at Lois Lane when the math started making me dizzy. Or halfway through History class, I might sneak a look at the latest issue of *The Fantastic Four that* I jammed in between the chapters, chapters describing such horrible events, events like those that led our country into the Civil War or World War II. So, I could either feel depressed learning about slavery in 1863 or ecstatic by sneaking a peek into a 1962 edition of *The Fantastic Four* and study how *The Hulk* once again was saving mankind from itself!

So, I figured that if I won some new issues of Superman or Batman, they would actually help me stay focused in class, maybe even improve my grades. Talk about a classic win-win situation.

Heading down Sherman Avenue on our way to Billy's, we saw Bobby Four

Eyes (doubt he saw us) and Buck Teeth Brady (as always flashing the best smile ever) and Evelyn's brother Jerry Gibbons. They were sitting on Bobby's porch playing with his little puppy, but no one seemed interested in playing cards for comics. I really wanted to get more guys to play, meaning bigger pots to win, so I pushed our best sales pitch. " Bobby and Jerry I know you are both basically blind but Billy's bringing some Playboy mags with centerfolds big enough to make your eyes pop out," I yelled as loud as I could, but Jerry just cried back, "Sorry, Sammy got tickets to see King Kong Vs. Godzilla, so I'm out," Jerry moaned, "but please can you win me some Playboys?" he laughed.

Shit, now I realized that we missed last week's Saturday Matinee and the coming attractions for this week's feature movie at the Warner, so I had no idea that King Kong Vs. Godzilla was finally out. I also had no idea if King Kong knew what he was getting himself into picking a fight with a 300-foot version of the Dragon from Sinbad The Sailor. Billy thought that since Godzilla looked like a Dinosaur, there was no way he could box with King Kong, not with his 5-foot T-Rex arms.

"Sammy, Kong can stand way back backup even further dance all around, jab him senseless, until he nails him with a KO uppercut."

I reminded Billy that Godzilla was 300 feet tall and had Atomic Breath. He could stand so far away that Kong couldn't reach him with a giant stick-ball bat, never mind with a left upper-cut. Then, he could just blow Kong a fiery goodbye kiss that would cook King Kong's ass.

Well, I thought, no cards for comics next week. Next week we will all be standing in line for some popcorn.

We did not even get to Billy's or start dealing, and I was already looking forward to next week, to King Kong, Godzilla, and popcorn. But that was next week. I knew Mrs. Heffern would have Hot Dogs, Peanut Butter and Jelly, and lemonade, so all we needed now was some candy.

So, one half block from Billy's, at the corner of Sherman Avenue and Second Street, we stopped at Harry and Molly's candy store to stock up on candy cigars, some real one cent Lucky Strike loosie's, Twizzlers, and a ton of penny candies.

"Do you really think Billy will bring some of his Dad's Playboys?" Pete asked while Molly kept her eyes glued on me, making sure no Hershey's kisses wound up in my pockets. Molly, who lived upstairs from her corner grocery store on the corner of Second Street and Sherman Ave., was about a hundred and fifty years old, just slightly younger than most of the groceries that she sold to our parents. The store itself was hardly as big as my family's kitchen, but every inch of every shelf, including the icebox, was filled with cereal, soup, eggs, milk, and ice cream. The whole store was only about 20 feet wide and 20 feet long, and when Molly was at the cash register Harry, her husband, did not take his eyes or knuckles off of us, making it a little harder to get our hands on those loosies.

When it was crowded as it usually was and the gang stopped in, the Moms and Dads would have an even longer wait as Harry would stop handing them Cheerios and immediately start to shadow us, especially when Frankie and Charlie snuck in with us. It was so busy because just about every family and kid from East Newark would walk over to Molly's at least five times a day. Moms would pay for the milk and eggs, and Dads for The Star-Ledger and the Observer while we went to play the nickel pinball machine and shoot our way to free penny candies and stink bombs. But as tough as she tried to be, and she was tough, even when the Pinball game ended in a tilt, Molly would still give us a Turkish Taffy or a fart bomb!

As much as we loved Molly when she was working the register, we had to be just as polite and careful when Harry was on the job because you did not want to mess with Harry! If Harry could survive six months in a camp with Hitler - a feat that he reminded us about daily - we figured he could probably handle a few crazy 10-year-old East Newark kids. We had heard enough of his stories about torture, especially how, at the end of the War, he got out of camp and ten-seconds later kicked a few Nazis in the ass. So, when Harry was at the register, most of us didn't even think about pocketing a piece of Pez or a Twizzler. Well, on second thought, Charlie and Frankie might've thought about it; well actually, they still tried.

"Mrs Molly, can I please see that box of Wheaties?" Pete asked, pointing to a box so covered in dust that you could hardly see the picture of Lou Gehrig, the 1936 American League MVP on the package. (Just as Molly started to wipe the dust off Lou, Frankie and Charlie snuck in, looked around for Harry and not seeing him headed over to load up the Pinball machine. Molly obviously knew what might be coming next, because before they could pocket some Pez and become pinball wizards, or even end the game with a tilt, she threw us all out the door.)

Pretty much every time Charlie and Frankie stuck their noses in the store, Molly would ask them to get out (Harry would kick them out.) Sometimes they were out the door even before they got their mitts on the Atomic Fireballs or shoved 20 penny candies into their back pockets.

"Guys! Looks like our ride to Billy's is finally here," I yelled as we were all being kicked out of the door. Our preferred ride around town, the Coca-Cola truck, was parked right in front of Molly's, and the driver was nowhere in sight. So, we jumped onto the rear fender and held on tight, waiting for the engine to roar and our ride to begin. As we waited on the bumper, the Coke driver loaded about 10 cases of Coke bottles onto his hand truck and started down into the basement through the cellar door. He seemed to be almost laughing when he stopped, smiled, and yelled, "Harry, are those rats still in the basement?"

A few weeks ago (according to Billy's Mom), the Coke driver came running up the basement stairs pushed open the cellar door and hysterically described how he avoided being bitten by rats, but could not avoid stepping in their poop! Harry laughingly blamed the driver for scaring them out of their rathole and for scaring the shit (that he stepped in) out of the rats, but he also apologized broke out a shoe shine kit and waxed-up the driver's Penny Loafers.

"I'm thinking he just pulled up a second ago cause he hasn't even started the delivery?" Charlie wondered aloud while adjusting his butt to fit the bumper.

"Yeah, I think he did," Frankie nodded, adding, "and it doesn't look like he's in a hurry to deliver Coke to Molly or to the rats either." We were sitting on the bumper to get a ride around town, not just to sit and watch the Coke guy make his delivery. After sitting on the bumper of the still stationary truck for a few minutes, we jumped off and started running down the three blocks: this was not as scary and certainly not as much fun as riding the bumper, but at this point, a lot quicker way to Billy's.

"I hope we get a ride on the truck later," I confided to Frankie.

"Where you want to go?" Frankie asked while laughing at my excitement.

"I don't know," I muttered, "but I have a few places in mind."

"Pete, what the hell is so funny?" Pete was laughing his head off all the way down Second St., showing off his toothless grin (and if Bobby Kreese hadn't already knocked his teeth out with a fastball Charlie would have)!

Finally, at Billy's, Pete dropped the grin and got serious about playing, taking out the cards one by one, and going over all the rules.

Pete always did this, despite knowing that he was the only one who knew the rules, paid any attention to the rules, or might actually follow the stupid rules.

Party Games

And then, just as we settled into Billy's backyard, out of the kitchen came his mom, pink apron on, drinks in one hand, chips in the other. As she put the lemonade and chips on the picnic table, I started smiling, and Charlie began dealing.

Frankie, as usual, came to the table empty-handed; no cash no comics, but between my Monster Mags, Pete's Superheroes, Billy's dad's Playboys, and Charlie's Archie's, we were ready to start betting. The comic that really stood out was Pete's 1958 Superman Vs. Batman, 25 cents special edition. I think everyone had their eyes on it, and on the Playboy's, I know I did.

My favorite games were seven-card stud and straight poker, Pete and Billy preferred straight poker, deuces wild, while Frankie and Charlie liked to mix it up by making up the game and rules as they dealt.

When they were dealing, four Kings might become four duces, or a full boat could capsize and become a sinking ship. It all depended on what wacky rules they dreamed up.

After about twenty hands (with either Charlie or Frankie caught cheating in nineteen of them), Mrs. Heffern brought out peanut butter and jelly sandwiches, and we agreed to deal one last game. Ante in would be five comics with a three-comic minimum per bet. No bumping up the pot until the last card was dealt.

I looked at the table and thought out loud,

"Holy crap," I yelled, "someone's going home with a hundred comics," and I was so sure it would be me I asked out loud "who will help me carry them home?"

"I don't think you will need a hand at all Sammy boy," Frankie answered even louder. Then, he named the game, seven-card stud and set the rules, jokers are wild sixes get an extra card, then he cut the cards, ready now to deal the last hand."

"OK, deal me in," I Anted up my five comics, said a prayer, and started biting my nails.

After dealing two cards down and one up, it was Billy's bet. "I bet three, who's in?" he asked as he pointed to Charlie and to his own King, the highest card showing.

"Billy, you think anyone is dropping out because of a King showing?" Charlie laughed while tossing a Wonder Woman and two Spidermen onto the pile. After dealing three more face-up cards, Billy had the best hand showing, a pair of Kings Ace high. Charlie showed Jacks, Frankie had Queens, Pete Duces, and I had a couple of Eights. We were all in! Billy dealt the last face-up card, and the final round of betting began. First, Billy bet three more comics, Charlie bumped him ten and Pete looked at his deuces did some math and dropped out. Billy still looked like the winner now with Three Kings showing, Frankie had Queens and Nines and a Six on the side. I had Eights, and Charlie showed Jacks, but we also both had a Six on the side so we would each get an extra card. My bonus card was a Duce, which was as helpful as a fringing Goose, so I folded.

"Are you in or are you out, Frankie?"

"Charlie, are you in, or are you out?"

Billy's extra card, a Seven, did not seem to help him either. But boy oh boy the way he kept repeating in or out had me thinking he's trying to get Frankie and Charlie to fold.

Then as Frankie dealt himself his extra card,

(I swear from the bottom of the deck) he started to go nuts as another Queen gave him a full boat, the winning hand, and about one hundred comics.

After we stopped arguing over the fact that we let Frankie in the game empty-handed, stopped laughing at the fact that for the first time, his schoolbag was full of books, and concluded that I should have called him out when I saw him dealing from the bottom of the deck. (For the 10th time) we agreed to trade comics till everyone had a few old favorites back.

Only then did we head back to my house, back to 533 North Third Street. Walking back up, Sherman Ave. We each made a few more trades: A Batman for a Justice League, two Supermen for one Spiderman, six Justice Leagues for a Playboy. Somehow, as always, we all left the Cards for Comics game with some old faves and some new faves.

"I guess someday I'll read Tolstoy Homer and Hemingway, but even if they are all they're cracked up to be, I doubt I'll

ever need/have a special hiding place for Tolstoy Homer and Hemingway as I will always have for my comics."

(Please Mom DO NOT throw away my comic books.)

CHAPTER 3

Roof Over Your Head

"I know it's important to have a roof over your head, but back in the day, it seemed more important (and way more fun) to have a roof under your feet."

East Newark New Jersey, in the summer of '62, the days seemed to last forever: no school, no summer camp. (That was for the rich Kearny kids.) No trips to Disneyland, a week down at the "Joisy shore" in July or August? Definitely! So many choices: Keansburg, Wildwood, Point Pleasant, Seaside Heights! But until we got to the shore, we honestly didn't think much about the beach. We needed to focus every minute on exploring EVERY inch of EVERY block of our hometown. I mean, we only had 15-hour days, because every day our Moms would say, "Boys get home as soon as it gets dark!" So, we absolutely had to focus on our town because sometimes, not often, but sometimes something around town just might change.

It was Saturday, June 22 (my birthday), and like most days, we headed north on Sherman Ave to the corner of 4th and Sherman. But unlike most days, we didn't stop at The Arrow Tavern (Boy! Talk about change) but at the Ure Inn. To us, the Ure Inn was still the Arrow Tavern. At least it was right up until this week when my dad (for some reason) rented it to Bob Ure, and he changed its name to The Ure Inn. Usually, we just walked in the back door, straight into the kitchen, and started shoveling coal, firing up the coal ovens to help my dad heat up the pizzas. Instead, today we nicely knocked on the tavern's front door, then as soon as Lefty the bouncer/bartender opened the door we ran inside. That's when Charlie grabbed his crotch, and asked for the first (but not the last) time, "Hey Lefty, does the Ure

Inn have a boys room? Cause I really need to take a leek!"

After we got kicked out by laughing Lefty and a ludicrous looking Uncle Louie, Charlie, also laughing out loud and underestimating Pete as always asked, "Pete don't you need to take a leek to?"

"Nope, Charlie, I need to do number two. I'm going down the block, down to Winnie The Pooh Inn."

"Where is that, Pete? Is that another new bar in town?"

"No shit, Charlie. You honestly really don't know where the Poo Inn is? Ask that Harrison kid, Christopher Robbin, he'll tell you."

"Christopher Robbin? Pete, I don't know him. Does he go to St. A's or Holy Cross school?"

"He goes to High School," Pete said to Charlie. "Someplace you'll never go!"

Back outside, still behind the Ure Inn, past the picket fence separating the two yards, we could see the giant oak tree in my back yard. It housed the treehouse that Uncle Louie helped me build (I did all the hammering!). Sitting 20 feet off the ground sat the six by six-floor, (no walls or ceiling) of the tree-house, right behind the treehouse, we could see my house, its roof, and the attic window. I was staring at the at-tic window, thinking out loud, when I blurted even louder, "Hey guys, you wanna go roof climbing?"

"Yeah, let's go, Sammy Boy." Pete was usually on top of things, and he was undoubtedly ready that day to climb on top of every roof on 3rd Street.

"I've got my climbing shoes on!" Charlie yelled barefoot yet happy to take the first step. But first, we would have to get up into my locked attic, the place where Mom kept all her stuff.

"Hey, Mom, can we go hang out in the attic?"

"OK, I guess so? Sure. What are you going to do up there?" "Well, whatever you do, don't you dare open the box with my wedding dress!"

"Just gonna play with the old toys and games," I yelled from the top of the stairway. As soon as Mom found the skeleton key and opened the attic door, she went back to making meatballs in the kitchen. "OK, have fun up there just don't forget Uncle Piggy, Aunt Lizzie and Aunt Lucy are coming over later, meatballs and gravy at three, oh, and before you go up please go see if the milkman stopped by yet."

My Mom was clearly happy in the kitchen making meatballs, while praying for our family, and for everyone who ever knelt on the pews at St. Anthony's church. Otherwise, she might have joined us in the attic. Joined us reading Monster Magazines and battling with Mr. Machine. Luckily for us, she was happily making the meatballs, because within five minutes we tossed aside the Monster Mag's, turned off Mr. Machine, and squeezed our little butts out the attic window.

After climbing out the attic window, onto the attic porch, we stared down and dared each other to jump off the roof, drop 25 feet straight down, and land in my four-foot deep backyard pool. Luckily, for once we just laughed at each other instead of taking the crazy dare.

We always began our long, fun journey to the end of the block from my rooftop, climb up one side of a roof to its peak, then down the other side. Jump the three feet between roof edges, trying hard not to look down at the 25-30-foot drop to the alleyways. From roof to roof, to roof from the top of my house to Mrs. Reilly's to Ronnie Cat's ending at the end of the block down at Mrs. Mary's on the corner of Third Street and Davis Ave.

Frankie always led the way, climbing up from the edge of every roof to its peak, then sliding slowly down the other side, to the opposite edge. At the brink while we were looking straight down 30 feet at the alleyway's below, Frankie usually pretended to push us off each roof into the alleys beneath us just as we looked down. He would scream out "look out below," and we all jumped with our eyes closed over the three feet between gutters onto the next neighbor's shingles. To get to the corner of Third and Davis, we would have to climb up and down seven roofs, jump over six alleyways, including the Cappuccino's four-footer, until we reached the twenty-foot drop to Mrs. Mary's flat garage roof. Then all we had to do was climb down Mrs. Mary's fire escape, jump down five feet onto her garage, hang on to the side of the garage roof, let go, and slide down the last three feet to ground zero, the corner of Third and Davis.

Getting to Mrs. Mary's was not always fun; it could be kind of scary climbing over Mr. Grouchy's house when he was home. I mean, he wouldn't even let us cut through his yard when we took the low road through town. None of us knew Mr. Grouchy. We just knew he fought in WWII, beat up some Nazis, came home and beat up his wife, and now lived all alone. We would tiptoe when climbing over his property, figuring if he heard us on his roof, he might shoot us like we heard he did the Nazis.

At the top of most roofs, we would sit with our legs spread, our butts evenly split between each side of the peak. Toes on one foot pointed to the last alleyway, and the other toes pointed in the direction that we would jump next. From the tip of the rooftops looking west, we could see the famous falling apart ONT building (that our parents called the Clark Thread Company). Way over the ONT and on the other side of the Passaic River, we could see all the truly nifty stores on Broad St. in downtown Newark.

If it was a sunshiny day, we could see for miles all the way down to the corner of Broad and Market St. We could see Klein's, McCrory's, and Hahne's. We would wonder about our next family trips to our favorite department stores to get slingshots, maybe a Hula Hoop, and hot dogs from the street guys.

That summer, on the day after my birthday, we sat on my roof, and before we even started our climb, Frankie (*who seemed a little bored*) looked down, turned around, and climbed right back through the attic window.

"Let's go climb up to the roof of the ONT. We can do a freaking ten block expedition, all on one roof!"

Frankie had me and Charlie so excited, so pumped, we looked down and almost took our 25-foot daredevil short cut from the attic to the pool. Luckily, Pete stopped us before we even came close to jumping off the roof. We followed Frankie back down the attic stairwell, through the kitchen where Mom was making perfect meatballs, and on to the front porch. Once we all got off the porch down to street level, we sprinted up Third Street down Sherman Ave, climbed over the steel fence, around the ONT, and saw that the last section of the fire escape that rose straight up to the sixth story roof came to a halt 12 feet above the ground.

Charlie came up with an idea so smart we could not believe it was his. "We can tie a brick around a rope, toss it between the last few steps, and pull the last leg of the ladder down."

We got a brick from the crumbling ONT, ran to get a rope from Pete's garage, and had the stairs pulled down to the ground in twenty minutes. Climbing up the six stories to the roof was a little scary (just don't look down), especially for Pete, but we all made it to the top and now stood atop the highest roof in all of East Newark, Kearny or Harrison.

The only problem was that we could hardly see anything except the sky and the ONT walls. The roof of the building sat 4 feet below the top of the surrounding walls. One block away from the East Newark jail, now somehow, we are trapped in 600-foot jail yard 70 feet above the ground. We did find some windows on the roof, that Pete told us were called skylights. Yet looking down through them, we sure didn't see the sky or any lights. All we saw was a ton of factory space without factory workers: no desks, chairs, workers, or secretaries. The top floor of the ONT was 100 percent closed. No one was weaving thread at the Clark Thread Company.

"OK, let's climb back to earth," I told Charlie, and we made our way about 55 feet down the fire escape, but somehow someone shoved/folded the last section back up. So, we were stuck on the fire escape at least 10 feet above ground zero.

We waved and yelled, "Hello, howdy, hey, is anyone down there?" but no one was walking by the old abandoned factory on a crappy Sunday afternoon. We tried dropping stuff (rocks and a soda bottle that we found on the stairs) to see if maybe we could safely jump off the last 10 feet, but the sound of the breaking Coke bottle convinced us it might not be a good idea. Then we saw God Damn Mike, our least favorite East Newark police officer, sitting in his cop car across the street laughing his head off. "OK, so now we know who folded up the stairs." We all knew who Frankie was talking about, but what we did not know was if God Damn Mike would let us down any time soon? Or, more likely, would he somehow really let us down by making us stay up there all day?

After about an hour of yelling and begging, Officer Mike walked over to the fire escape, looked up, smiled at us, and promised: "I'll let you down in time for Sunday dinner, but don't you ever climb up that roof again! Got it, guys?"

"Never again, Officer Mike," I said and thought (well, at least not till next week).

"I always looked forward to Mom's Sunday Pasta, but never more than I did on that Sunday when we spent an hour on the edge of the Passaic River sitting 10 feet above our home ground, with the ONT roof 55 feet over our heads." Come on; Mom bring on the meatballs!

CHAPTER 4

Senate Boys Pool Room

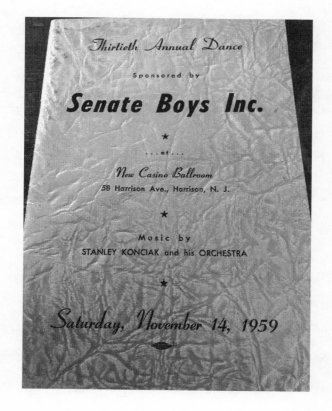

Thirtieth Annual Dance

Sponsored by

Senate Boys Inc.

★

...at...

New Casino Ballroom

5B Harrison Ave., Harrison, N. J.

★

Music by

STANLEY KONCIAK and his ORCHESTRA

★

Saturday, November 14, 1959

"What was the most fun at the Senate Boys pool room? It wasn't the pinball machines, pool tables, foosball table, or even the free pizzas, it was watching and listening to the guys, to Tootsie, Peppy, Lefty, Shorty, Big Moe, Jimmy the Wig, Gino, Mr. Bones and all the rest of the gang."

A few days after our O.N.T. fire escape adventure, we were right back on our steady ground headed south down Central Ave. We were about two blocks from Tops Diner (the best and only diner in East Newark) when Charlie spotted the Coke truck parked outside of Spinnely's sweet shop.

Just as the driver was finishing up his delivery, Charlie whispered. "The last one on is a horse's ass." As soon as the Coca Cola guy jumped back into the driver's seat to cruise to his next stop, we jumped on the back fender and hitched a ride down Third St. to the pool room, (officially known as the Senate Boys Club). Just as the driver pulled into the pool room parking lot, we hopped off the fender, saw that Lefty was working the back door and knew we could walk right in. If Tootsie was at the gate, we had to try and sneak in or get Mr. Shortie to convince Tootsie we were only going to the backroom to do our homework. When Lefty was at the back door, the rule was we could watch the poker games, play the pinball machines, buy sodas and chips, if we stayed away from the pool tables. However, unless Tootsie was around, Lefty never paid any attention to that rule either.

I remember one Sunday I challenged Stevie Kramer to a game of eight ball, nickel up winner gets a dime, and as usual, Stevie wanted to up the ante before we even broke the rack. Our parents all said Stevie had Polio. All we knew was that Stevie's left leg was about a foot shorter than his right, and even his peculiar shoe with the 6-inch sole did not get him close to level, so he hopped around like a bunny rabbit while playing Eight-ball like a pro. Stevie would prop his left leg up on a little step stool, sink the five ball drill the six and seven balls chalk up his cue stick jump back on the stool focus on dropping the Eight-ball while I reached in my pocket for the dime I would soon owe him.

It was after losing a few hundred games to Stevie, and it did not matter if we played eight-ball, nine-ball, or straight pool I could not beat him. Then, and only then did I figure out that my only chance to win was to make up games with MY! Rules. Rules like you could only hit the eight ball with your eyes closed or by substituting your middle finger for the cue stick. Ouch! The crazier I made the rules, the better shot I had at winning and getting my dimes back, (at least that's what I thought). Only Stevie really didn't care what stupid rules I came up with; he would just laugh and say, "OK, rack em up," just before clearing the table and pocketing another dime. Even when I made a rule like all shots must be taken with two feet flat on the ground, he would still give me a run for my money.

Another thing about Stevie was that he had the weirdest laugh ever. Whenever me or Charlie would do something stupid (which was pretty often), he would snort so loud as well as tilt his head up and down so we could see up his nose. It was not pretty, but it was funny, and for all of his limping, hopping, and snorting Stevie more than anything else was a lot of fun.

As much as I liked Stevie, Pete loved him much more, and even though Frankie and Charlie couldn't beat him in eight or nine-ball (so sometimes they busted his balls), we were all friends. Well, the guys in our gang were.

Some of the older Harrison high school kids, especially Ronnie Cattana A.K.A. Ronnie, the Cat, were really mean to Stevie they would snort his name and ask him if he needed a "Polio stick" instead of a Pogo or a cue stick. Sometimes Stevie would just ignore them; other times, we would all tell them where to stick the sticks.

"I'll tell you where to stick it, Ronnie." Shouting out loud like I often did on the phone, "Up yours, Cat-man."

Walking around town with Stevie could be an adventure. Sometimes, if he forgot his crutches, he would step with his left foot (the one with the shorter leg) on the curb and his right leg and foot reaching down the curb onto the street leveling things out for a while. Level, at least until he hit the corner of the block or a bump in the road. Stevie never ever complained about his shorter leg, and within the gang, his leg stood out only as much as Charlie's half-inch index finger, Pete's missing teeth or Bobby four-eyes' six-inch thick glasses.

Stevie always seemed disappointed when I told him (after mass, after hours of shooting pool and after 40 cents transferred into his pocket), that I had to go home for the other official version of Sunday mass, Sunday pasta! (Disappointed, yeah but only until I invited him and Charlie over for meatballs.)

The day after that Sunday, like most Monday's it was a full school day, but this Monday (like many others), I had to spend one hour apart from my Fifth-Grade classmates. I was sent to Second Grade because Sister Mary Anthony caught me shooting a rubber band at Janice Mathewson. Luckily, she didn't see the note I handed Janice five minutes before class, asking her for a smoochie, cause that would have broken all the rules. I also would have spent a lot more than an hour in second grade had Sister Mary Anthony caught me, Charlie and John, kicking each other before lunch, or everyone copying John's homework before Math. (John being Mr. smarty pants, A.K.A. Mr. know it all, especially when it was time for Math.)

Sometimes me and Charlie or even Dennis would spend a whole day in Second or Third grade depending on what we got caught doing! Or not doing! Like our homework. It could be a lot of fun to sit with the little squirts in Second grade relearning the alphabet and reading Little Bo-Peep, but it did make it even harder to take the Fifth-Grade math test the next day.

I really didn't enjoy studying fifth grade Math or Science and was sometimes caught reading the Superman comics that I stuck between the multiplication and division chapters. However, for some unknown reason, I was beginning to like fifth grade more and more every day. I found myself shooting fewer spit-balls and even fewer rubber bands at Charlie and more and more trying to focus on Science, Sharron, and Janice.

I learned in a hurry that Janice preferred that I pass a note to her front-row desk rather than shoot it at her with a rubber band from my school desk in the back row, (the A Plus kids sat in the front row). I even tried to move my school desk up a row, but Sister Mary Anthony reminded me that if I wanted to move from row C to row B, I would need to get B's on my report card. I started to figure out that the only way to sit next to Janice or Andrea Latini, would be to work a little harder in class and on my homework. (But I was still wondering why I wanted to sit next to them so badly?)

Occasionally in class, my thoughts would go back to an episode from Dobie Gillis, a show that my sister Dianne and I watched on our 13-inch black and white T.V.

In this episode, Dobie was as always deep in thought, sitting next to the historical statue of Rodin's The Thinker while pondering aloud about his feelings for Mary Ann. How can I grab her attention? Should I ask her to the movies? Or to the school dance? He wondered and wondered aloud; meanwhile, in almost every scene, after every question that Dobie asked himself, Mary Ann, in a close-up, and as if reading his mind crinkled her nose, raised her eyebrows, frowned, smirked and laughed at Dobie just as often as Janice did to me. At the end of the episode, Dobie sat with The Thinker both deep in thought. The Thinker wondering about human nature and Dobie bemoaning the fact that while he could not quite get his arms around her, he also could not get Mary Ann out of his head.

"Brown Eyed Girl" by Van Morrison was the first song I could not get out of my head, and Janice was the first girl I wanted to get my arms around, and just like Dobie with Mary Ann I could not get Janice out of my head. One day after class, while Van repeated the chorus, over and over that went something like this (My brown-eyed girl, you are my brown-eyed girl), I asked blond-haired girl Janice if I could walk her home. No cards for comics, no roof climbing, not even a stickball game was set up, so while Janice was asking me something about our homework (why she was asking me I'll never understand), I awkwardly mumbled, "Can I walk home with you?"

"Really, Sammy, you're asking me to do your homework?"

"No, I didn't say anything about homework, I am asking if I can walk home with you!"

By now all the other 5th graders were halfway up the block. Janice answered me by picking up her bookbag wrinkling her nose and walking backward uphill on Sherman Ave away from me and St. A's heading home. I caught up quickly, and when we got to my house halfway into the five-block walk, I tossed my bookbag on my front porch and offered to carry Janice's the rest of the way.

"Whoa Janice, how the hell do you carry this?" I guess it made sense that her school bag was a lot heavier than mine. After all, it had our math, history, and science textbooks in it. Common sense? I guess so since Janice always did all her homework. I usually did my own history homework, but almost always copied Pete's or John's science or math before class, so I never had to carry such a heavy load.

Walking down 3rd Street past Davis Ave and the East Newark public school playground, we saw my older sister Dianne staring at me, (as she loved to do) from across the street. "Sammy, where are you going?" I shut my eyes turned my head ignored her question and picked up the pace. I already could hear Mom in the back of my head, a half-hour before she even asked me: "Sammy what were you doing with Janice, where were you going, why didn't you say hi to Dianne?"

Hmmm, "Oh, now I remember Mom. Janice and I were thinking so hard about one of the intros to algebra problems the one that's in tonight's math homework, that I didn't even see Dianne."

"Intro to algebra? Wow, I'll tell your sister to go over it with you tonight."

"No, no, that's OK I'll go over it in the morning with John."

We made the left turn off 3rd Street onto Central Ave. Now officially in Harrison, we walked past my buddy Johnny Cinardo's house before stopping at 328 Central Ave right in front of Janice's front porch. As we walked by Johnny's, I was actually glad that for once, he was not winding up on the sidewalk pitching to the porch wall expecting me to be his catcher.

I sure liked walking Janice home, and I sure knew why I did, (well I thought I knew why), but once we got to her porch, I was frozen. I put her bag down, mumbled something about homework, thought about holding her hand, then took turns looking at her smile, at the sky, and at the ground. I also had a great idea about asking if she wanted to go to the movies, then started cracking my knuckles and scratching my nose, I thought about giving her a big smoochie, then began whistling Brown Eyed Girl. Time stopped. I looked at her; she looked at me. I tried to say something, but my tongue was tied, and Janice's eyes were rolling. Finally, after standing in front of her house for what seemed like an eternity, she threw her arms over her head and blurted out.

"What... What... What, Sammy, what do you want?" Then she grabbed her book bag, started laughing, waved goodbye, and left me standing confused and speechless in front of 328 Central Ave.

Back in Third grade, I would never have even thought of walking Janice or Andrea home. In Seventh grade, I sure did think about it (actually, in Seventh grade, I did more than think about it.) In Seventh grade, I stopped twiddling my thumbs and tried unsuccessfully, wrapping my thumbs, hands, and arms around Janice. But in Fifth grade... Well, I guess in Fifth grade in 1962, I really did not totally understand why I wanted to walk Janice home?

*(What was the most fun at the Senate Boys pool room?) It wasn't the pinball machine's pool table, foosball table, listening to the guys, or even the free pizzas. Actually, in 1962, the most fun was **walking past** the Senate Boys pool room, walking past with Janice, pondering over, and wondering why I had, and what to do with, **both my twiddling thumbs and pounding heart!***

CHAPTER 5

Mischief Night

While the summers seemed to last forever, when September was over, and October arrived, we saw less and less of the fruit truck on Third Street and started to see Pumpkins on the porches. Pumpkins? What could be more fun than a Pumpkin?

One Saturday in October of '62, me and Charlie were sitting on my front porch (when my Dad yelled out, "Get the hell out of here, get moving! Go have some fun"). Never ones to ignore our parents, we started looking for a little mischief, and knowing we could find it anywhere started looking everywhere. Well, everywhere to us meant all-over our three-town universe.

While walking from my home base on 3rd Street in East Newark, we were getting excited about the cherry bombs and fart perfume that I saw on the Wildwood boardwalk in September, the ones that my mom promised, (and I made her swear to Jesus) she would buy for me next year. I figured the wait would be worth it cause, for now, we could make just as much mischief at The Arrow Tavern in Harrison by leaving a few worms on the bar. Or if we were in Kearny by tossing a rubber puke gag into The Argyle fish market, or the best prank ever drop a bag of fake poop right at the front door of

Molly's candy store in East Newark, and watch her open it!

Somedays I had no idea if we were Pogo sticking in Harrison or kick balling in East Newark but we did know we might get lost if we crossed over the railroad tracks into Newark, or even worse, get stabbed with a sharpened tree branch in a sword fight with the crazy Kearny kids. A duel that would start sometimes, well almost every time, we walked fifty feet onto and over or under the bridge into Kearny. But this Saturday, just after leaving my front porch and beginning to wander all of a sudden and from out of nowhere, Charlie seemed to know exactly where to go, a light bulb lit up over his head, pointing us in the opposite direction.

"Let's head down to Mrs. Murphy's, she might have some free Pumpkins."

"OK, but what do you want Pumpkins for?"

"Just thought of a really cool idea when your Dad kicked us off the porch."

"Can you share it?" I asked Charlie. I was thinking about last year when we tossed a few ripe ones from my roof after Halloween.

"Hmm, I'll let ya know after we get em, I'm working on two plans, hmm, one of them I think will really bowl you over!"

"Bowl me over? Charlie, what the heck are you talking about? You mean it will knock me out?" I, as usual, had no idea what the hell Charlie was mumbling under his breath.

"Does one of the plans include dropping a Pumpkin and turning it into a squash?"

"Nah, we did that last Halloween, anyway, let's go to Mrs. Murphy's."

Not a store or a kids' lemonade stand, Mrs. Murphy's porch was more like an adult lemonade stand. Mrs. Murphy would either sell or give away penny candies, frozen juice bars, popcorn, or handmade sweet drinks depending on her mood or if you had any nickels or dimes in your pocket. Charlie, (who rarely ever had even a penny) stopped getting free candy last summer.

Why, because one afternoon after pleading poverty as always, he got a few freebies, ate a few M&M's and then while still chewing was ratted out by a Harrison High kid. Mrs. Murphy instantly forced him to empty his pocket's, revealing a dime, two nickels and four pennies. As far as I can recall, that turned out to be the last of the free M&M's for Charlie. Sorry Charlie, better luck next time. I remember Mrs. Murphy telling Charlie after he got ratted out just to be honest, and next time he might get some freebies again. To this day, I'm not sure he totally understood Mrs. Murphy's good intention or learned a life lesson because years later, he told me that from that day on, when he did have some change, he hid it not in his back pocket but in his sneaks.

No free Pumpkins at Murphy's (or anything else that day), but we did get two nice sized ones for no charge from outside of Dennis Hock's (another one of our fifth-grade classmates) garage.

"You really think Dennis won't care that we took 'em?" Charlie wondered out loud. (We did knock on his door to see if he wanted to join us for some fun, but no answer.)

"Nope!" Charlie answered his own question, "Not when he finds out what we did with his pumpkins. Then he will just be really pissed off that he wasn't home when we came knocking."

So, pumpkins in hand we made a U. Turn, headed back up Central Ave, peeking into the windows of every bar and family store, noticing that most of them already had some Halloween monsters inside creepily staring right back at us.

As we cut through East Newark (took almost five minutes), I could see the light bulb over Charlie's head flashing even brighter. (I always envied his smile as much as I did his athletic talent) but right now, I just really wanted to know what the hell was behind that humungous great big smirk!

"OK, so where are we headed with our nine-pound pumpkins?" I asked as we turned onto Hamilton St. crossing back into Harrison.

"Well, we could go to your roof as usual, or to Yeager's? I'm thinking Yeager's!"

"OK, Yeager's it is."

The fact that we skipped past my house two blocks back without Charlie even looking at the roof, made it obvious that my rooftop was not in the plan we were going to Yeager's.

Yeager's was a bowling alley on Hamilton Street, right across the street from the Harrison kids grade school. It had a little hot dog and burger stand, a make it yourself seltzer and syrup soda bar and it was also a big hangout for lots of dads in the so-called beer and bowling league.

Not only was Yeager's popular with all the bowling moms and dads, but it also had some fun after school jobs for the high school guys, especially the crazy pin setter job! We knew that the new bowling alleys like the one's on Harrison Ave and on River Road in Kearny had some kind of super-fast pin setting contraption that picked up the pins you missed, swept away the pins you bowled over, then reset the ones you missed and even rolled your ball right back in the gutter to you. Kind of a reverse gutter ball. Except at Yeager's all that was still done by the High School pin setter.

Because of the Pin Boys it was way more fun at Yeager's Lane where in any 10 frames I could roll at least five gutter balls, two or three strikes, and try once every few frames (or watch someone try) to bowl over the pinsetter. Being a pinsetter (Pin boy) seemed like a really fun after school job, even if sometimes some nutty high school kids or fifth graders from St. A's tried to strike them with a slow roller while they were trying to reset the pins. I think they realized it was part of the job, and it was probably covered in the half-hour job training.

Yeager's had four lanes, and after school and on weekends, all four lanes had a pin boy, and on the weekends along with the pin boys, they always ran a real special deal five-ten frame games for only one dollar. But I knew neither of us had a buck, and I doubt Charlie even had twenty-five cents for one game.

"OK, Charlie, I really don't feel like going bowling, so why the hell do you want to go to Yeager's?"

"To strike a pumpkin if we are lucky, or at least squash some pins, I'm still working on the plan."

"OK, we're here now what's the plan?"

Charlie did not answer; he just opened the door and ran, and as always, I followed, past the soda jerk, past the hot dog stand right up to lane number one where we stopped, and Charlie shouted out loud.

"Hi, it's me, Peter Pumpkin Eater!"

Mr. Borghesi, (Mr. B.) was standing just behind the foul line waiting for the pin boy Blackie Tomczyk to finish setting up the pins when Charlie jumped in front and with perfect form rolled his pumpkin, full speed, at the ten pins just as Blackie changed lanes. Not to be left standing in lane one holding the evidence, I ran over to the next lane, way past the foul line, and heaved my nine-pound pumpkin at the 10 pins sitting at the end of lane two. I have no idea if I bowled a strike, or rolled a gutter ball? Because within seconds Blackie, Mr. B., and about 20 other dads and moms were laughing out loud, while chasing us across lanes three and four, around the pinball machines, back past the hot dog stand and past best friend Pete (looking at us with a smirk and some envy). We ran out the front door right back onto Hamilton Street, hid in Mrs. Davit's backyard for five minutes, snuck out, and headed for home.

With October almost over and with pumpkins and scary monsters now on just about every porch in town, we all started to think more and more about the most fun night and day of the year, Mischief Night and Halloween.

"Should we practice like last year?"

Frankie had come up with a great idea last year to go to the houses and stores (a week before Halloween) that already had a lot of Halloween decorations, knock on the doors and say, *Trick or Treat now and next week!* A lot of neighbors just laughed, but some also gave us tiny treats and said they sure hope to see us in full costume next week. So, it was no surprise this year that a few neighbors were actually expecting us, seemed glad to see us and not at all stingy with the treats.

The simple fact is that *Trick or Treat now and next week* went as well again this year as did the real Halloween. That made it kind of a no brainer even for Pete and me that Frankie's new idea that he told us about the day after Halloween "*Trick or Treat got any leftovers?*" might fill up the bags a 3rd time even though Halloween was over and the monsters were leaving the porches.

A few days later after mass, lunch, and changing out of our Sunday best, we met in front of Molly's figuring that would be the perfect place to try the new Trick or Treat leftover plan.

"Sammy, you never talked about wearing our costumes again?"

Charlie was surprised that I had my Dracula fangs and cape back on.

"I know, I forgot, but just in case you didn't wear em, I brought my sister Dianne's lipstick with some fake teeth and noses for you guys."

Charlie looked even scarier than on Halloween with the lipstick on his nose and eyebrows and teeth coming out of his ears, but Molly did not seem afraid at all just confused.

"Wait a minute wasn't Halloween just a few days ago? Oh, I get it, Trick or Treat got any leftovers? Hilarious boys!"

Instead of just giving us M&Ms, Hershey's Kisses, or just kissing us goodbye, Molly gave us each three free turns on the penny gumball machine. With each of our three free spins, there was as always a One in a Million chance that the gum-ball you got would be the Giant Red One marked LUCKY, and Harry would let you the start picking your Twenty-Five free penny candy's.

After all of our free spins with nothing to show except regular gumballs,

Charlie told Molly his last turn got him the winning Giant Red Lucky gumball but that he ate it by mistake. Harry did not get mad; he just smiled, looked inside the gum-ball machine, saw the LUCKY gumball, and told us to make sure our Moms and Dads stopped by for their daily shopping. Then he tossed us all out.

Molly's sure gave Trick or Treat leftovers a great start, and after knocking on about five neighbors' doors (the ones that still had decorations) and a few other Mom and Pop shops, we decided to head over to the Arrow Tavern. My Dad was probably making Pizza in the kitchen when Lefty the bartender told us there wasn't any more candy, but the few guys sitting at the bar around 2 PM on Sunday afternoon threw the five of us a few pennies and nickels each!

"50 cents at one bar, holy crap lets go to Bobby's Bar next." Frankie was looking scary and feeling filthy rich, and even though Charlie said he only got one penny and one nickel (we figured the other ones were in his back pocket), he still ran with us to Bobby's.

Bobby's wasn't a restaurant/bar like my Dad's Arrow Tavern. No pizza just shots and beers, and free pretzels for the guys at Bobby's.

Knock-Knock "Yeah, what the heck do you kid's want?"

"Trick or Treat got any leftovers?"

"Get the hell out of here. Why aren't you at school?"

Not sure if it was Bobby or one of his lunchtime beer buds, but in so many words, he told us to get out and go back to school. No school on Sunday, but we did get the hell out, I slammed shut the bar door behind us, and we all laughed when Frankie pulled out Dianne's lipstick and scribbled on Bobby's front door CLOSED ON SUNDAY'S!

We were almost to Mike's Deli when a Harrison Cop car pulled up, and the officer told us all to hop in the back seat. He said that he got a call from Bobby's Bar and that we were all under possible arrest for suspicion of damaging his property. Five 10-year-old's fit pretty snuggly in the back seat, and in less time than it took to get us in, we were pulling into the back lot of the police station. My Uncle Vinnie, Chief of Police in Harrison, brought us into a back room closed the doors stared at me and told us Officer Mike would be gathering our information in five minutes.

Charlie and Frankie were pretty sure because my Uncle Vinnie was the boss; we would be let out no questions asked.

"I don't know Charlie, I think Uncle Vinnie said God Damn Mike [our nickname for officer Mike] would be getting our info in a little bit?" I had no idea if Uncle Vinnie would just let us go, but I was pretty sure he would rat me out to my Dad either way.

John and Pete were pretty scared, both knowing what would happen if their Moms or Dads found out. John had already removed his scary nose and wiped away the lipstick around his eyes, ready to tell officer Mike he was just an innocent bystander. Pete was basically shitting in his pants, his teeth (the few he had) were chattering, and hot sweat was dripping from his nose when officer Mike walked in the room with pencil and notepad in hand.

He asked each of us for our full name address where we went to school, the grade we were in, and our teacher's name. After penciling in all our info, he asked a few last questions.

"Any of you boys ever been to a police station before, and are any of you known by another name, a secret name, an alias?" "OK, let's start with you," Officer Mike said, pointing at Pete.

"My name is Peter Borghesi... and..."

That's when Pete's breathing got quicker, his teeth started to shatter out loud, and he almost caused a flood with his sweat.

"What is it, Peter? Do you have something to tell me about your record? Have you ever been arrested anywhere before? Do you go by a secret name? Or do you have an alias?" Officer Mike inquired, looking right at Pete, looking really worried for Pete, and he seemed genuinely concerned about what he was about to find out. "Peter again, do you have an alias?"

"My name is Peter, but uh… my, my friends, uh, my friends. Ummm, my friends they.., they. My friends, they call me ummm, my friends they call me, uh… they call me PETE!"

Officer Mike was now almost laughing. "OK, you guys go right the hell home, stay out of trouble, or next time I will have to call your parents."

"So, while summer did not really last forever, it just really seemed to, it sure was true that nothing and I mean nothing could be more fun than a Pumpkin."

CHAPTER 6

A Jimmy Boyer Night

How to start the weekend?

"OK, let's walk over to Mike's. He should have the new Justice League and Fantastic Four comics, then we can meet Charlie at Spinnilie's for a soda pop before we check out the new Two Guys From Harrison store. Oh, I forgot, I told Frankie we would meet him at Mollie's so let's start there."

Me and Bobbie Ferrero were about halfway across Third Street when Mrs. Boyer yelled down to us from her second-floor bedroom window. "Three packs of Lucky Strikes boys, keep the change," and tossed a dollar bill wrapped around a few Hershey's Kisses.

"OK, Mrs. Boyer, I'll stop back in 10 minutes."

Frankie was sitting on the gutter outside of Mollie's, so I got the Lucky's from Mollie, and we ran over to Mike's corner comic store to see if there was a new issue of Batman and Robin or if Betty and Veronica were still fighting over Archie.

We knew we could get three new eight-cent comics with the 19 cents change from the cigs and tax's because Mike would collect the other five cents from one of our Mom's when they stopped by for Time magazine Newsweek or the

Star-Ledger. "Thanks, Mike, see ya next week."

Walking down Central Ave, we saw Charlie sitting on the curb outside Spinnilie's. "I guess Mr. Spinnilie's going to Aqueduct today," Charlie was reading the note stuck on the door next to the Coke sign.

(CLOSED NOW! OPEN TODAY AT FIVE)

Mr. Spinnilie (when he was at the shop) was always on the phone with my dad betting on a parley (Giant's+10 Packers -7) or going over the odds for that day's races at Belmont Park or Aqueduct Raceway.

"OK, well, I guess soda pop at five," I told Bobby as we headed over to River

Road in Kearny. "Let's go check out the new Two Guys. I think it's finally open."

Two Guys from Harrison was a little Mom and Pop (or Pop and Pop) store in Harrison that closed down a few months ago, kind of like a slightly bigger version of Harry's and Molly's in East Newark. Since it closed, our parents talked a lot about the new department store being built, also called Two Guys from Harrison, that was being built in Kearny, which made no sense at all. We knew all about the brand-new store being built because the construction was across the street from our sleigh riding park on River Road. One day last winter, after sliding to the bottom of the snow-covered sled slope, we threw some snowballs at a worker driving his tractor and almost shit in our pants when he turned the tractor around, picked up speed, and drove straight towards us. Lucky for us, he stopped just in time to not run us down but close enough for him to toss some snowballs right back at us.

If we never stopped tossing snowballs at the workers, they would never get back to work, and Two Guys even though it's closed would remain one of our favorite Mom and Pop stores, but we were told if we stopped tossing the new store would soon be the first, the only one and our favorite department store in East Newark, Harrison, or Kearny. Because there were so many department stores in Newark we really didn't need another one so we kept tossing snowballs at the workers slowing down the construction and keeping our arms in shape. Of course, eventually, it stopped snowing; we stopped tossing snowballs, and now here we were walking from Spinnilie's through a giant parking lot with every spot filled. Every parking spot was leading us to a giant glass door that opened all by itself into Two Guys from Harrison department store smack down in the middle of Kearny.

"Escalators, wow, Sammy, did you know they would have escalators."

"I did Bobby, my mom told me Two Guys would be 2 floors."

We had all seen escalators before, Haynes department store in Downtown Newark had some, but these were brand new shiny and really steep. "Hop on," said a worker telling us where the toy department was. So, we headed up, hoping they had the new *Rock Em! Sock Em! Robots*. We were almost to the second floor along with about twenty adult shoppers when suddenly, the escalator came to a screeching stop, half the riders falling forward, knocking over the rider in front of them. Instantly a siren started blaring, and an overhead light started flashing. Once everyone was off the escalator, a store worker started asking everyone what happened and if anyone was injured or if anyone pushed the emergency stop button? Everyone on the escalator seemed fine yet scared to hell by the lights and sirens. It was only after the manager told the worker to silence the siren and restart the escalator, and the 200 shoppers that ran out of the store were assured they were safe and started shopping again that Frankie confessed to us what he did.

"I just kind of had my toes squeezed against the moving stairs, just as the top stair started to go into the ground, I felt my whole foot being crunched. Then all at once everything stopped, and the screeching started. I really have no idea what the heck I did."

Frankie was as always totally puzzled, yet Bobby, whose dad was some kind of an engineer, did seem to know what happened and said the best way to see if it really was the foot jam that stopped the escalator was to try it again tomorrow. So, while we never found any *Rock Em! Sock Em! Robots*, in Two Guys that day they did have *The Atom Bomber, Pogo Sticks, and at least* a ton of *Super Balls*, and we were 100% sure and excited about tomorrow when they just might have another store evacuation.

"Meet at Molly's tomorrow after mass?" Bobby was already thinking about another trip to Two Guys as I waved bye and walked up the steps to my front porch.

"Sammy, what's that in the bag?"

"Oh, crap, I forgot to bring the Luckies to Mrs. Boyer."

I ran over and knocked on Mrs. Boyer's door, but no one answered, and she was not looking out her second-floor window as usual, so I figured I would just bring them over tomorrow after mass. A little later, when Mom and Dad were at The Arrow, I was sitting on the couch with my sister Dianne watching Abbot & Costello when Jimmy Boyer, who was a 15 or 16-year-old Harrison high school kid showed up at our front door and asked for his Mom's Luckies.

"Got the smokes, Sammy?"

"Yeah, I got em in my room, come on in Jimmy. I'll grab 'em, you know I tried to bring 'em to your Mom, but she was not home."

"Whatever," Jimmy said, seeming a little pissed. "Just give me the Luckies and the change."

"I don't have the change, we bought some comics, Jimmy. Your mom always lets us keep the change."

"Yeah, when you go to Mike's and come right back and give er, her smokes, not when she has to wait eight hours for them."

"OK, Jimmy, come over later when everyone gets back, and I'll give you the three packs, and my Mom will give you the change."

"Nope, I am here right now, and I'm sure you can find a few pennies somewhere."

Jimmy was right about that, Uncle Louie usually had one or two pairs of pants hanging on the door, and it was OK to take any pennies, nickels or dimes from his pockets as long as I told him when I did.

We went into my bedroom, the one me and Uncle Louie shared since I was a one-year-old. I gave Jimmy the Luckies, grabbed Uncle Louie's pants hanging on the hook on our bedroom door and emptied the pockets. I was hoping he had some change, but all he had, was a bunch of dollar bills, some fives, and a ten.

"What about that other pair hanging in the closet?"

"Nah, I grabbed the coins out of those pockets this morning before we went to Two Guys, the only thing left in those pants is bucks. I promise I'll get the 19 cents from my Mom or Dad when they get home."

"You better, and next time just go get my mom her Luckies and bring em right back got it?"

"Got it, Jimmy."

"OK, I'll give my mom her cigs and tell her I'll get the change tomorrow. I'll go out the back door is it open?"

"Yeah, wide open it's never locked unless we know Aunt Lizzy is coming over. She goes crazy when we leave the doors open, always tells us how the bums from Newark can walk right in, in the middle of the night. So anyway, I guess I'll see ya tomorrow? So while I was excited about going back to Two Guys after mass I was not looking forward to seeing Jimmy Boyer again!"

A few hours later, after dinner and laundry, Mom whispered, "Sammy, it's almost 10 o'clock! As soon as the Abbott and Costello show is over, turn off the T.V. and go to bed, Uncle Louie is already sound asleep."

"Why, Mom? There's no school tomorrow."

"Cause we are going to early mass and then walking to grandma's."

"Mom, but I'm going to Two Guys tomorrow."

"We'll be back right after a late breakfast with grandma probably before noon."

"OK, I'll call Bobbie in the morning and tell him to make sure the guys wait for me."

Uncle Louie was snoring away on his bed, and just before falling asleep, I noticed the alarm clock on the nightstand between our twin beds was set for 7:30 AM, pretty early for Sunday, I thought maybe Uncle Lou is coming to mass with us? I whispered, "good night Uncle Lou," said my prayers, climbed in bed, and pulled the covers over my head.

In the middle of the night, I was sound asleep when some squeaky noise woke me up. I stuck my head out from under the covers and froze! Someone was standing by the closet, quietly opening the door on Uncle Louie's side and reaching for and sticking his hands into his jackets and pants pockets. I could not move an inch, say a word, I was paralyzed from head to toe.

It's fucking Jimmy, I could not have been surer it was him even if he was wearing his basketball jersey with Boyer on the back. I tried to scream out to Uncle Louie and grab his arms, but my lips were numb, and my arms were frozen. I watched as he grabbed the bills from Uncle Lou's pockets and stuck them in his, then started to open our dresser draws. I tried as slowly as I could to slide my arm six inches over to the night table and grab the alarm clock, and when I finally did, I flipped it right at Uncle Lou.

Ring, Ring, Ring, the alarm clock's clang broke the silence at two in the morning sounding ten times as alarming as it would've at 7:30 AM, and I noticed that along with the silence it almost broke Uncle Louie's nose.

Jimmy started running through the kitchen towards the back door as Uncle Lou began calling, yelling, "Moe, Moe, get up there is a fucking robber in the house."

"Dad, it's Jimmy Boyer, it's Jimmy Boyer!"

Jimmy was barely out of the alleyway when Uncle Lou and my Dad opened the front door, ran onto and off the front porch, and started chasing (in their underwear) Jimmy down Third Street. (Uncle Lou had long black boxer shorts, but Dad was sprinting after Jimmy in tighty-whities and a Guinea Tee!) My Mom was now wide-awake standing on the front steps holding the house phone at the end of its fifty foot cord trying to call Mrs. Boyer and the East Newark cops. Within 15 minutes, both Mrs. Boyer and Goddam Mike were all on the porch when Uncle Lou and my Dad were turning back onto Third Street from Sherman Ave. After putting on some pants (Uncle Lou's missing a little cash), they all headed back down Sherman one block to the E.N. police station. My Mom was holding Mrs. Boyer's hand the whole time while officer Mike was asking her where Jimmy was all night and where he might be now?

After officer Mike walked back to the police station, Mom was back home in five seconds. After checking in on me, and my sisters Dianne and Lois, she put me back in my bed and, with tears running down her face, asked.

"How did you know it was Jimmy? Sammy, are you certain it was Jimmy?"

"It was Jimmy Mom, I knew it was him the second I saw his scared shitless face staring at me in my bed at two in the morning. The room was really freaking dark, but the corner of the closet where Jimmy was standing was lit up by the moonlight coming through the bedroom window, and when the alarm smashed onto Uncle Louie's nose and started ringing Jimmy spun around and stared right at me for what seemed like an hour."

"He hit Uncle Louie with the alarm clock?"

"No, I did Mom, that's how I woke him up and got Jimmy to jump out the door. Mom, he looked like he saw Frankenstein, but before Uncle Louie even got out of bed, Jimmy was out the door."

"Sammy, Mrs. Boyer said it was definitely not Jimmy, even though she does not know where he is tonight?"

That's when I told Mom about going to Mike's for the three packs of Luckies for Mrs. Boyer and how we wound up at the Two Guys grand opening, that I totally forgot about the smokes, spent the change and how much that pissed Jimmy off. Then I told her the rest of it, about Jimmy stopping by when she was at The Arrow and how he stood almost precisely in the same spot in my room eight hours ago and watched me go through Uncle Lou's pockets looking for the change I owed his Mom, and how I found only bucks. "Mom, then, when he saw me shove the dollars back into the pockets, he nodded and said OK." I even confessed that I told him our back door was hardly ever closed and rarely locked, well unless Aunt Lizzy was over.

"You told him we never lock the back door? What the hell were you thinking about."

"I don't know mom I thought he was just asking if he could go home out that door, not if he could come back in at two in the morning."

I didn't see Jimmy B. again until years later. Although I sometimes saw Mrs. Boyer sitting on her porch smoking her Luckies, she either walked to Mike's deli or he brought them over and shoved them into the mail slot in her front door, cause she never asked us to go to Mike's or tossed any candy wrapped in a dollar bill down to us again.

We were told that Jimmy was sent to a reform school, whatever that was, and while a few high school kids mentioned his name, they never saw him either. I guess the reform school was pretty successful because when we finally did see Jimmy again about six years later standing on his front porch, he was surrounded by and being loudly cheered on by about 25 friends, family, and neighbors. Jimmy dressed in full uniform was being cheered, saluted, and given thanks for his six months service in Viet Nam!

I, however, still had some evil thoughts about Jimmy and did not even think of saying anything to him about his being a hero, or talk to him about and bring up that night six years ago, or how I still thought he was a real Jerkoff.

It wasn't until I ran into him again a few years later when I was home for a few days after my eight weeks of basic training, and the country was so torn up and divided over the Viet Nam War that we actually spoke. I never did time in Nam as we started bringing home the troops the very week I was drafted. Still, I did begin to grow up and learn enough about his service and commitment to the country to forgive Jimmy. Forgive Jimmy for making my Dad my Purple Heart, Silver Star, Bronze Star award-winning WWII hero Dad chase him around town in his underwear six years ago, and to thank him for his duty.

I had no idea that what started out as a regular weekend, ya know cards for comics and soda pop at Spinnilie's, would become a weekend I'd never forget. I do know that emptying every customer from Two Guys was fun, what a blast, but Jimmy Boyer evacuating my house in the middle of the night was not so much fun, unforgettable memory but not much fun!

CHAPTER 7

Back in Town

"Not sure reform school was his preferred first stop, but Jimmy did what me Charlie, and most of the guys were trying and hoping someday to do. He got the hell out of town. 1st stop reform school? 2nd stop Viet Nam? There must be an easier path? But the Army did get Jimmy out of town; maybe my route would be baseball? Could I turn a Home Run into a runaway from home?

Curb ball was my favorite/best street game, my worst was basketball.

I was also good at stickball, punch ball and backyard baseball. So, I got really jealous when Bobby Ferrero told us he was signed to play on the Harrison VFW Little League baseball team. I had walked past the Harrison Little League field many times on our way to Grandma's house but never when the teams were playing or even when they had practice. I didn't even know East Newark kids were allowed to play in the Harrison league. That Saturday, after Bobby told us he was playing, I watched his VFW team beat the Elks Lodge 16 to 11 and watched Bobby get two hits, field three grounders, and pitch an inning.

"OK, Bobby that really looks like fun, how the heck can I get on the VFW? Or even on the Moose?"

Bobby knew I was a better hitter and faster runner than he was from all of our stickball and backyard baseball games. Yet, on the other hand, I had never played on a real baseball field or team.

"Let me ask my Mom and Dad. They know the coach of my team."

"Thanks, Bobby, and I am going to ask my Mom to take me to Two Guys after lunch and buy a bat and glove."

"I know coach Davit said we need a first baseman."

"I'm not getting a first base glove; I want to play centerfield like Willy, Micky, and the Duke."

"OK, Sammy, I'll tell my Mom to ask coach Davit what to do."

"Thanks again."

Bobby's Mom gave my Mom Coach Davit's number, and she called the coach a few seconds later. Ten minutes later, he had me running the bases, fielding some grounders, chasing some fly's, and after taking some BP told me. "Get an outfielders glove, Sammy."

"Like Willy's and Mickey's right coach!"

"And the Duke's. That's right Sammy, welcome to the VFW team next game is Saturday at 1. Make sure you get to the field by noon! Noon got it?"

I got to the Harrison Little League field Saturday at 11 before anyone from either team, and started to wonder if I got the day/time wrong? After a few other parents and players finally got to the field, Mom left the bleachers and started walking past home plate on her way to Grandma's.

After the Star-Spangled Banner was played, the Umps yelled play ball! And my VFW team took the field while I sat along with six other teammates on the bench. I was twiddling my thumbs and holding my pounding heart while trying to soften up my new glove by stretching and sitting on it and slamming a ball into the pocket. The game against The Moose was tied four to four in the bottom of the fifth inning when Bobby and Joey both walked and advanced to second and third on a wild pitch. With 2 outs, Johnny Cinardo blasted a single, and we were winning 6-4. The Moose got the last out in the fifth, and we took the field in the top of the sixth (last inning) up by two runs.

I was still hoping to get in the game, but all my fingers were almost without fingernails, and my heart was still pounding when the Moose Lodge loaded the bases with no outs.

"Bobby, off 3rd base, go to the mound Tommy, take over 3rd Sammy center field Mike, you go to right field."

With those changes, Coach Davit had emptied the bench and shifted his best pitcher from third base to the mound with three outs to go and the bases still loaded.

"I'm finally in a game, and I am in center field, and I don't have my fucking glove!"

I was so freaking excited and, at the same time so nervous about being on the field, being a real part of the team, actually in center field on my first day on the squad. So freaking excited that I ran to center field as fast as I could the second I heard, "Sammy center field," but without my goddam brand new glove.

"Holy crap don't hit the ball to center." I hid my hands behind my back while sweating, biting my lips and yelling. "Strike em out Bobby!" At that point, I didn't care if Bobby walked 4 Moose in a row, and we stepped off the field losers as long as no-one hit a fly ball to or a grounder through the infield into center field. I wanted to run off the field find my Mom in the stands and never play in another Little League game, but she was nowhere near the field or in the stands (still at Grandma's, I guess).

Bobby took a deep breath and started mowing down the Moose. After striking out the first batter, he faced their best player Joey M. Joey Ripped a liner to right field right to Mike, who snared it after diving about 3 feet towards the right-field line. I saw the ball roll out of Mike's glove drop onto the grass under Mike's belly, and so did the Moose coach who came running out to argue the call with the umps. I guess the ump did not see the ball pop out after the great catch, (I barely noticed it from 20 feet away) cause he stuck to his call, and so did the home plate ump.

After the Moose parents screamed for the umps head and the coach did the same, he was told to leave the field and join the Moose fans in the stands.

Now with 2 outs, Bobby got the next batter to hit a high pop behind Johnny at second and if I had my glove, I would've called I got it. Instead, I ran right around Johnny, our 2nd baseman, not even watching him make the catch straight into the dugout.

Game over.

I never showed up for another game that season or signed up to play Little League again. I never got over the feeling I had standing in center field that day feeling naked and afraid that someone might hit the ball to me.

Mom just figured I really did not want to play, and my Dad was much happier and more likely to be lying on the couch watching the Yanks with me on TV than to ever go to any Little League games.

Another blown chance to get out of town, All-Star games in North Arlington, away games in Ironbound, Little League events all over the state. Walking home that day after my one inning nightmare in my only Little League game, I was thinking even more about getting out of town when I ran into Charlie in front of Mike's deli.

"Hop on, Sammy."

Charlie was sitting on the rear fender of the Coke truck waiting for the Coke driver to finish up Mike's order when I jumped on, and the driver pulled away.

After a few stops at Molly's and Spinnillie's, Frankie joined us on the fender as we headed toward Top's Diner on River Road. After the Top's Diner delivery, we were headed back into Harrison on 2nd street when we made a weird turn just before Cleveland Ave and Joey D's bar.

"What the hell?"

"Where the heck are we going?"

Frankie was flipping out as the Coke truck suddenly was picking up speed going a lot faster than the usual 10 15

MPH he went on the streets of East Newark and Harrison. That's when we saw the giant signs declaring the Grand Opening of Route 280. We had seen the signs and saw the workers for years but had no idea it was going to be a real highway! Within 20 seconds, we were on the bridge over the Passaic River, looking right at some of the giant apartment buildings next to downtown Newark.

"Oh my god, jump off Charlie," I yelled and jumped as the Truck was now turning onto what was I guess Route 280 picking up speed by the second. Charlie and Frankie landed two-seconds after I did on the muddy, grassy side of the highway entrance. We all crash-landed, rolled about 20 feet, and scraped every inch of our skin, blood was pouring from my lips and nose and Charlie's forehead. Frankie couldn't even get up, it looked like he busted a foot and bloodied his hands. Charlie helped Frankie limp back over the bridge, and we headed straight back to the Spinnillies soda shop. When Mr. Spinnillie saw us bloodied and limping into his shop, he looked right at me and said.

"OK, Sammy, now what the hell are you guys up to?"

Mr. Spinnillie called our parents, and we all went to Dr. Kellerman's office, got cleaned up stitched up, and later told all the guys about the new way to get out of town, Route 280!

Although baseball did not turn into my way out of town when I was 10 years old,

I still love it and started playing again when I was about 14. I have been playing on, coaching, and running baseball and softball teams now for over 50 years. I have been to tournaments all over the East coast, once even beating Trinidad and Tobago in a softball championship game in Cleveland. I have also traveled to Major League games all over the East coast. But back when I was 10, it wasn't baseball; it was the neighborhood Coke Truck that first got me out of town!

CHAPTER 8

The Arrow

7th grade has been OK, I guess, but to be honest, the best week of 7th grade so far was the week I spent in 4th grade. Sister Appolonia sent me to 4th grade for a week after I kept pretending to be dead when called on in class to give the answer to, "What is the capital of North Dakota?" Or "Who was the father of our country?" I really liked the fact that the other kids got a good laugh out of it. Still, sometimes I pretended to sleep because I really had no clue about North Dakota or any idea who the hell the father or mother of our country was. I did know that my father fought in WW2, was awarded a purple heart, a bronze star, a silver star, fought/sparred with the heavyweight champ Joe Louis, and was known around town as Big Moe. Now he runs the Arrow Tavern, where I am known as Little Moe. I have often been asked why I am called Little Moe? (because I was Big Moe's son) and just as often how my Dad got the nickname Moe in the first place? Even my Dad didn't really remember, but of course, Pete knew.

"Sam, your dad got his nickname the same way Tootsy got his."

"Oh, now I understand, thanks, Pete."

In 1958, when I was 6 years old, St. Anthony's school in East Newark started with only one grade, our class of nine-first graders. The entire school was the nine of us and two teachers. Every school year beginning in 1959 when St. Anthony's added a grade, we moved up a class, so I was always one of the biggest, toughest, and except for Math, Science, English and History, smartest kids in our school. In 1959 St. A's had 17 students, and we were the second-grade upperclassmen bossing around the new first graders. Now it's 1964, somehow, I've made it to 7th grade, one of six 7th grade boys, and the whole school has almost 100 kids.

I love St. Anthony's School and church, especially the church after altar boy practice. That's when we go down to the holy bargain basement and see old statues of the Saints, we were especially excited to see St.Lucy, her eyes torn out of her face resting on a plate as if she was offering them to the poor. Or of St. Thomas with that doubting look on his face, or statues of Joseph and Mary with the lambs and sheep standing around the empty Manger that longed to hold the bargain basement, Jesus. It was last year that the bargain basement Jesus was promoted, and he now lies in the crib on the main altar right next to the wine and hosts. I don't know whatever happened to the Baby Jesus that used to rest in the Manger upstairs, but the one from the basement filled in nicely.

As much as I loved St. A's, by Fridays, I couldn't wait until we got out of class, away from Sister Pasqual, away from the church, and away from Father Joe, or as we called him, Holy Joe. Holy Joe would say mass, preach about sins and forgiveness and then curse out the altar boys, Pete, Charlie, Billy, or whoever was working the altar that day. Curse us out for fidgeting during mass and spilling either the water or the wine depending of course on how far along the mass was.

Not that Friday was all that different (it didn't matter if it was Monday or Friday) I wasn't thinking about homework or penance, I was thinking about what we could do when school let out. And what the weekend had in store for us.

Pete B. was my best friend. We did all kinds of stuff together, play ball, go to the movies, play cards for comics, even hang with our parents. But when I stopped by his house that Friday his Dad said he was busy, yeah sure, most likely busy doing Math home-work. Anyway, when Pete was busy, and I wanted to do some fun stuff like go from 533 north 3rd Street to 551 north 3rd Street by jumping from roof to roof over the 3-foot alleyways be-tween houses. I could always call on Charlie or Bobby cause they were for-ever up for crazy stuff. If I thought it would be a good idea to put some dog poop on Mrs. Riley's porch, ring her bell and run like hell, Charlie might suggest putting it in a cute little gift box or in a bag labeled "surprise!" No matter what I thought of Charlie would always come up with some bet-ter, funnier, nuttier ideas.

Bobby F. was my little friend from two doors down on 3rd Street. He was only in 6th grade in the East Newark public school but was a fun kid and a fantastic baseball player. Bobby not only made the Little League all-star team, but his parents actually went to his games. (My mom sort of went to my only game.) He could also pogo stick down the block with no hands, with one foot, or with his eyes closed, almost as fast as I could. I think Charlie is actually a little jealous of Bobby or does not like hanging with a sixth grader because when he calls Bobby, it's always. "F! Bobby, Not Bobby F." Then when Bobby would get mad, Charlie would grin and say, "Bobby F., what the F are you mad about."

My answer to Charlies question every week was always "I don't know what

Bobby's mad about but I know I'm mad about his sister Lizzy." And I think it will always be the answer, well, at least as long as Lizzy lives two doors from my house at 529 north 3rd Street.

After Friday's basketball practice, we were officially done with school, so Charlie, Bobby, and I met at Molly's candy store to figure out our plans. While we were getting some penny candies, Charlie looked at me with his usual grin that told me something good was coming. Charlie then tilted over the candy machine, trying to get some pennies to fall out. He would try this just about every week, just before Molly straightened out the candy machine picked up any pennies from the floor and threw us out.

Last week, when she threw us out, we were laughing so loudly we never even heard the 6 o'clock Our New Thread factory whistle blow letting us know the factory was closed for the day. Walking towards the Our New Thread building A.K.A. the O. N. T., we planned on climbing up the fire escape and onto the 60-foot high roof. However, two cops, including Big Mike, who we called "Officer Shit Head," were sitting in the only East Newark cop car right in front of the O. N. T. having coffee and doughnuts. Still, we tried to sneak up behind the car to get under the fire escape, but Big Mike, his mouth stuffed with doughnut dough flashed the lights, sounded the siren and pointed us away from the factory. Within minutes, Big Mike was back to sipping his coffee, so we ran from the O. N. T. parking lot, took a short cut across the railroad tracks, and headed back up Sherman Ave to my Dad's tavern, The Arrow.

The Arrow is one of about 5,000 bars in a one-mile radius in East Newark and Harrison. Usually, every block had two bars at each intersection and one in the middle of the block. Some cross streets have one on every corner plus a few in the middle of the block. But the Arrow is not just a bar; it's also a pizzeria with a dining room, pool tables, pinball machines, plus the infamous backroom for the guys and their card games.

The guys are a mixed bunch. Some hardly look much older than us. Well what I mean is they don't act much older than us, though some are as old as my Dad, and some are even older. One thing they all seem to have in common is that they don't have regular names like Bob, Harry, Kevin, or even Mr. Pagano. But, if you were looking for Tootsy, Lefty, (no right hand) Peppy, God Damn Mike (AKA Officer Shit Head), Gino, Piggy (300 lbs), Moe, Shorty, (four feet 11inches) or Mr. Bones, (all 100 pounds of him), you would find the guys at The Arrow, or at Tootsy's poolroom almost every night, including Tommy Chicago and Jimmy the Wig (bald as an eagle).

Tootsy runs The Senate Boy's pool room down the other end of 3rd Street, it has lots more pool tables and ping-pong machines, then The Arrow and a giant backroom card table. The poolroom's a second home to a lot of the guys or a third home, depending on how much time they also spent at The Arrow. Toots, as we called him, always had a big fat cigar hanging from his lower lip, and even though there are plenty of spittoons in the poolroom, he somehow missed 'em with half his gooey gobs.

Gino is my friend Johnny Cinardo's Dad, and unlike most of the regulars at The Arrow, he seems to have a regular job, kind of like Mr. Cleaver on Leave It to Beaver. But Johnny was more like Dennis the Menace then The Beaver.

Mr. Cinardo might not always wear a gray suit flannel to work or take a train to Manhattan, and at the end of every working day, swing the door open and say like Mr. Cleaver always did, "Honey, I'm home what's for dinner?" But he does wear a tie and work in an office building in Newark, maybe for N.J. Bell? Selling life insurance? Or 64 Chevys? Mr. Cinardo is also one of the few Dad's we might see mowing his lawn, praying at church every Sunday, or at Mike's deli after mass buying groceries for his family.

God Damn Mike is an East Newark cop and a lot younger than most of the poolroom and Arrow crowd, but he sure fit in when it came to poker and betting. On weekends during the football season, God Damn Mike and my Uncle Vinnie were usually at my house in uniform, answering the phone and taking the bets. They gave the odds on Sunday's games while my Dad handled the day's results from Belmont and Aqueduct. God Damn Mike would bark out the odds, "Giants plus 7 you got it $20 on the Giants," or "You want to parlay Giants and Dolphins? Giants plus 7 Fish, minus 3 done deal."

My Uncle Vinnie, who is the chief of police in Harrison, and Big Mike usually have their police uniforms and badges on when they are on the phone taking bets. Although Uncle Vinnie always takes Big Mike's gun away before the games start because as big as Mike is, he has an even bigger temper.

Uncle Piggy got his nickname well, this is kind of funny, because, he kind of looks like Porky Pig, snorts when he laughs and weighs around 300 pounds. He sort of works for Frank E. Rodgers, who, if I can believe Uncle Vinnie, has been the mayor of Harrison for almost 100 years. Sometimes Uncle Piggy helps clean up after a storm or with the trash pickup, but mostly he just does whatever the mayor wants to be done. If the mayor needs help working the voting booths, Piggy's on it, handing out election flyers, he's on it, town parade or town picnic, paint the town red, on it.

Uncle Piggy and Mr. Bones are buddies, and it's always funny to see them together except if Mr. Bones is standing behind Piggy, then you can't see him at all. "Hey, what happened to Mr. Bones where the hell is he? where did he go?" goes the line repeated a thousand times. I have no idea what Mr. Bones does when he's not at the club, except sometimes when he is there, he sells all kinds of cool stuff from the trunk of his big 62 Chevy. Parents can get a toaster, a T.V., cases of soda, of beer or a transistor radio. We might get a baseball bat, ice skates, a pool stick, or a B.B. gun, but the best deal ever was a few years ago when I got a pogo stick directly from Mr. Bones' trunk on Christmas Eve.

Most of the other guys, Lefty, Peppy, Shorty, Jimmy the Wig and as far as I could tell, Pauli, work occasionally driving taxis or driving trucks. Trucks filled with stuff that somehow winds up in the trunk of Mr. Bones 62 Chevy for all the neighbors to buy at a steal. Some of the parents call Mr. Bones a fence, and Tootsy always smiles, spits out a gob, and laughs, "Yeah, he's as skinny as a fence post."

The one thing all the guys seem to have in common is that they all hang out at the pool room a lot during the day, especially on weekends and come to The Arrow almost every night for food, drinks, and some night's go back to the pool room for card games.

I like all the guys except Big Mike, who we are all scared shitless of. How he treats us kind of depends on whether any other adults are around or someone's younger brother or sister. If my Dad is in the pool room, I'm "Little

Moe," if he's not, I'm a knucklehead, or I just get to feel some of his knuckles hit my head.

Officer God Damn Mike likes to hang out by Top's Diner and not just for the coffee and doughnuts, but for its location next to the Clay Street bridge that connects East Newark to Newark. From his spot in Top's parking lot, he would check out just about every car that drives over from the Newark side of the bridge into East Newark. He tells the guys over and over, "Any Moulin-yan that thinks he can just drive into East Newark has a date with Big Mike." Apparently, Mike wants the people in Newark to hate him as much as most of the East Newark folks did.

After our day's unsuccessful climb up to the O.N.T. and some stickball, I knew it was getting close to 5 o'clock, so I figured we'd better get to The Arrow before it got too late to start working on our end of the deal.

East Newark, from one end of Harrison to the Kearny bridge, is all of 12 blocks. But still, I only needed the 3 blocks from the O.N.T. factory to The Arrow Tavern to fill Bobby and Charlie in on the deal my Dad had laid out.

My Dad, aka "Big Moe," is not only the only and best bookie in town, but he certainly makes the best pizza. Only Cerbone's pizzeria in Harrison even comes close, so this was a perfect deal. Usually on Friday night we would try and fold 100 pieces of cardboard into 100 boxes and usually make at least 90 pizza boxes, enough for the weekend's deliveries and pickups. Then we would fill the oven with coal, start the fire, and after Dad made the dough, cook the first pizza of the night. If we did it without burning down the Arrow, that first pie with the toppings of our choice (sausage, pepperoni, extra cheese) was ours to eat.

Now, Charlie was the last kid in town any adult would put in charge of starting a fire, so my Dad had Bobby get the coal from the basement and toss it into the oven. At the same time, I set a match to yesterday's daily racing form, burned my fingers, and cried out as I threw it on the coal. While I got the oven ready, Bobby went through the fridge looking for the best toppings for the first pie.

Left to twiddling his thumbs, Charlie started looking around and found a burlap sack of live mussels that had just been delivered. Out of sheer boredom, he asked my Dad, "Mr. Pagano, can I cut open this bag of mussels?" Dad looked at me like maybe he was thinking about what harm Charlie could do opening a bag of mussels. Dad then pulled me over and said, "Tell Chuck it's OK, but first tell him to put the bag in a bowl, put the bowl in the sink, and then open the bag in the sink." I yelled over to Chuck, "OK, Charlie, let's do it." But before I mentioned the part about the bowl and sink, Charlie cut open the bag on the floor, and we all started howling and laughing as one hundred spider crabs caught with the mussels escaped out of the sack and started scampering in a hundred directions.

Dad was har-haring as loudly as we were, but he stopped when Bobby opened up the swinging doors to the tavern. Those swinging doors reminded me of the entrance to the bar in the western show Gunsmoke. Just like the doors in Gunsmoke, they had a little gap on the top and bottom and would swing open all the time, usually when someone wanted to know if the drinks were watered down, or who won the 5th at Belmont. But tonight, the crabs finally saw a way out of the kitchen. I had seen the spider crabs before, but not so many, and I don't think even one crab ever made it out of the kitchen to the bar. But now, 50 or 60 crabs ran out the door while The Arrow regulars were pointing, laughing, and jumping onto the barstools as the crabs ran wild.

Little Stevie K. was next to one of the first barstools, shoeshine kit in hand, and despite having one leg a lot shorter than the other, sat very comfortably on his shoeshine box, giving Lefty a shine. It didn't matter if Stevie was hopping around the table, playing eight ball, or getting a 50-cent tip for a 25-cent shine. He always had a grin like a cartoon character, and he sure was grinning when the crabs started zipping around his shoeshine kit, the one he was using to polish Lefty's penny loafers. "Look at these little buggers!" He laughed and grinned as he reached for some crabs, tipping sideways towards his short leg while grabbing hold of Lefty for balance, accidentally getting black shoe polish all over Lefty's khakis, and then the grin was gone.

"You stupid little shit head. I'll break your other leg!" Lefty screamed as he pushed him away. Stevie tripped over the shoeshine kit and fell face-first into the barstool. The other guys in the bar were all laughing with Lefty until they saw the blood from Stevie's nose start to run like a faucet onto the floor of The Arrow.

After Stevie gathered his shoeshine kit and limped out, the rest of the guys started giving Lefty some of his own medicine.

"I'll bet $20, his mom will sue you!" Peppy howled while Bones gave Lefty a few shoves. "How do you like it? Huh, Huh, Huh? Picking on a little kid!"

"If she sues, I bet Lefty will be gone long before the lawyers figure it out," said Gino.

Since getting cancer in 1958, Lefty was known around town as "The Incredible

Shrinking Man," not only for losing almost 100 pounds but for how fast he was losing the 20 thousand dollars his parents left him. Lefty looked mad as he stormed out the door right behind Stevie, but I was sure we would see him again later that night since it was Friday, and that meant a poker game in the back room.

Things calmed down a little, so we started a game of nine-ball when my Dad (Big Moe) walked into the bar from the kitchen, rounded us up, and had us round up as many crabs as we could. Dad put us back to work, making pies when Charlie asked, "Why is the crust always so burnt on our pies?" Dad slapped his forehead, "Because the oven surface gets hot before the air in the oven does, so the first pie or two will always have a burnt crust. When the entire oven is hot all over, and the pies are cooked just right, then they go to the paying customers so until you guys have 75 cents for a large pie keep enjoying the burnt ones."

After we ate our burnt pie, The Arrow was coming back to life. The crabs were mostly gone, most of the regulars never left, and now the dinner tables filled up with local families and their little kids. Even Lefty strolled back in.

Dad was getting busy, so Bobby, Charlie, and I took off down 4th Street toward Harrison and the basketball courts. Charlie entertained us by singing the Who's latest single at the top of his lungs, "I Can See for Miles and Miles." He sang the chorus over and over while slamming his head into every other parking meter, telephone pole and street sign. Bobby joined Charlie humming along, making it a duet chiming in, "I Can See for Miles and Miles," but apparently, he really could see as his head barely kept missing the street signs. Every person walking on the streets, and I all liked Charlie's head-splitting version much better.

On the way to the basketball courts, we passed Mike's Deli, where Bobby's baby sister, Maureen, was cuddled up all alone outside Mike's in her baby carriage. We stopped to tickle Maureen when Bobby's Mom, Mrs. Ferraro, came out of Mike's. She handed us her groceries, pushed Maureen's carriage, and marched us back to 3rd Street and shoved Bobby right into his front door. So, Bobby would not be joining us at the courts despite his begging, "Mom, it's not even 6 o'clock!"

We got in a few rounds of 21, and played a full court game before the high school kids showed up and kicked us off the court. We would jump back on when the big guys were at the opposite end of the court, sprint under the hoop, shoot a jump shot and sprint off, sometimes Charlie would grab the rebound take a chance, and take another shot. After one of Charlie's layups, I missed the rebound, and the ball bounced right to Kevin Gilmore, a high school football player, as he was leading a 2 on 1 fast break, Kevin grabbed my missed rebound, gave me a stare, and tossed the basketball at me just like he threw a 60-yard bomb in the last Kearny game.

Kevin, the star Quarter Back at Harrison High, is headed to Marshall University in the fall, and as far as we know is a pretty good guy. Until I messed up his fast break, the only problem I ever had with Kevin is that he is dating Ronnie Cat's sister, who I kind of have a secret crush on. Once, when we were waiting for Ronnie Cat outside the Cat man's house, I told Charlie how pretty she was, and Charlie cracked, "Man, you just like her boobs." If Kevin heard Charlie's boob remark that day, he would have been pissed, but not as mad as he got when I messed up the fast break.

"Hey Pagano," Kevin called, "you and Charlie want to play in this game?"

"Uh, not really, Kevin, we're just shooting around."

"Shut up, you little dork face," Kenny N. snapped, grabbing me while Kevin cornered Charlie under the basket. He wanted to know, "Do you kids really want to screw up our game?" He was pissed, and even though we said sorry, Kenny, we soon found ourselves in the middle of a full-court dodgeball game. Kevin caught me with a 70 mph pass right to the head, and the blood from my nose ran onto my shirt as I wobbled off the court. Charlie dodged Kevin's bullet passes so well that Kevin had to grab and hold him while a few other high school kids kicked him in the ass. Charlie was not smiling for once. Well, that basketball game was over, so we decided to head back to East Newark and The Arrow.

Back at The Arrow, things were heating up. A few families were finishing their pizza, and a bunch of the neighborhood guys were doing shots and drinking beers.

"When you guys gonna play poker?" Charlie asked.

"Why do you ten-year-old punks got some cash to lose?" Laughed Paulie. He knew we just wanted to watch and maybe get a few tips for bringing the guys some beers from the bar so we could buy some comics from Mikes Deli. Paulie stopped laughing and shooed us away as he walked towards the back room, yelling, "Things will start wheeling when Moe starts dealing."

"So, dad, when will the card game start?" I asked. "When I stop getting orders for meatball sandwiches and pizza deliveries, but since it's Friday, I don't think that will be for another hour, at least."

"OK, daddy-o see ya in an hour." Heading down Sherman Avenue towards

St. Anthony's, Charlie was giving an encore performance of "I Can See for Miles," but without an audience it was apparent he really could see. Cause now he only slammed his hand into every tree on Sherman Avenue not once slamming his head as he did earlier. Did Charlie's vision improve? Or maybe he was getting a little wiser? Ha, ha, ha, I don't think so!

As we headed towards school, we saw Pete and Tony Borghesi tossing a football around in their backyard. The yard was also a parking lot as Mr. Borghesi had 6 garages behind his house. Mr. and Mrs. B. used two garages, and some other East Newark families rented the rest. The backyard was big and paved so we could play three on three basketball, ringolevio, box ball, or even three feet and a lead. But tonight, a little football would be fun. Whether I was running a deep route, a short shuffle pass, or a simple handoff to the fullback, Pete had the plays down. Not only was he the quarterback but the radio announcer as well.

"Charlie's going deep, he's wide open, but wait. Sam is closing ground. What a stop! Sam jumped 10 feet in the air to knock down the sure T. D. pass."

"It's second down Sam fumbles the snap; this could be a game-changer but wait, he bravely and insanely dives onto the concrete, rips his blue jeans, and re-covers the fumble!"

It was me and Pete against Tony and Charlie. After four quarters and well into sudden death, the score was tied when Charlie got wide open, but the pass from Tony fell short, and this time Pete made the interception while letting everyone in earshot know what a dramatic play it was. "This could be the game! Lombardi is wide open in the end zone! Wait. Borghesi's pass is short again, and Tony's little brother Pete steps in front with a clear pick before being pushed into the Cat Man's garage at the 10-yard line."

"That's enough of this bullshit, Tony. Take the damn plastic wrapping off the frigging ball!" Charlie had enough of Tony's strangeness. Tony was a little older than us, already in high school, and was famous around East Newark for a few funny quirks. On this day, the one that drove Charlie mad was Tony's refusal to take the plastic wrapping off the new football Mrs. Borghesi had just bought him from Two Guys. The fact that it was hard to catch and almost impossible to throw a good spiral did not bother Tony in the least. "The ball will be as good as new for weeks and weeks, and anyway, it's my ball," Tony giggled back at Charlie. At the same time, Pete and I recalled another funny Tony quirk, this one having something to do with his refusing to wear socks more than once.

Pete announced that the game would be halted because of darkness and would resume when Tony agreed to take the wrapping of the ball. "It will be baseball season before that happens," Charlie predicted. Game over. We all decided we better get back to The Arrow if we wanted to watch the guys play poker.

"Why? What's going on at The Arrow?" Pete asked. So, I told him about the poker game and what happened earlier with Stevie and Lefty. Pete was not surprised by the story. "Lefty's a ticking time bomb. He scares the shit out of me." Pete didn't hang around The Arrow or the poolroom like a bunch of my other friends, so he didn't always see the funny side of the guys. Also, he seemed to want nothing to do with a backroom poker game like me, and Charlie did.

Walking back up Sherman Ave., Charlie and I caught some fireflies, squished them around our fingers, rang some doorbells with our "fire" fingers, and ran like hell. We could usually run a half block away from a house before the neighbor would answer the bell, so we really didn't expect Mr. Riley to open his door just as we were ringing the doorbell two times. When we showed him our on-fire fingers, he was not mad at all and suggested we ring Mr. Murphy's doorbell next. As much fun as dinging and running could be, we called it "ding, dong, ditch," we were getting ready to watch the guys play a little seven-card stud.

The Arrow, on the corner of Sherman Ave and 4th Street, is firmly in Harrison. It's a full 50-foot walk to get back into East Newark and almost another 20 yards before stepping into Kearny. When we played football on the corner of Sherman, we often ran a play called three towns. Tony would snap the football to Pete in East Newark, Charlie could make a fake cut through

Harrison and catch the bomb on the bridge going into Kearny. Tonight, our pass route ended just short of the Kearny bridge at the front door of The Arrow, where we were greeted by Shorty, who told us my Dad had just started dealing in the back room.

The poker table was round and full of nuts, beers, and ashtrays, but for most of the guys, the floor was an ashtray. Dad had on his official poker dealer's cap with the see-through visor and a pack of Camels stuck inside his guinea t-shirt. Peppy sat with Mr. Bones, Tootsy, and Gino on Dad's left. Big Mike, Uncle Piggy, and Lefty sat to his right. Dad dealt the cards, and the winner of each hand would call the next game to be played. Seven-card stud, five-card draw, straight poker with deuces wild, or our favorite, Jacks or better.

The games were going along fast with lots of laughs, and the guys were throwing Charlie and me a few quarters for getting beers from the bar a cigar from Mike's, or even giving a buck if they won the last hand. As the pots got a little bigger and the ante kept going up, things started to get a bit heated around the table. Tootsy kept demanding the last cut of the deck, and Uncle Piggy wanted to quit while 50 bucks ahead. That's when officer Big Mike put his gun shooting finger to Piggy's head. "You're up 50 bucks. It's not even 9:00, and you want to go home? That's bullshit." I looked at Dad, and he called me over and told me things were getting a little shaky, and after the next hand, we would have to go home. I did not want to leave but then thought I might get back in time to watch Dobie Gillis get dumped by some high school chick again. Of course, I could watch Dobie only if Mr. Stupeillo finally stopped by with whatever T.V. tube he needed to fix our T.V. set that has been tubeless, causing me to miss Dobie Gillis for almost a week now.

Because Lefty won the last hand, the choice was his, and Lefty finally picked a game of Jacks or better. He seemed to be red hot tonight with a pile of ones, fives, and even a short stack of Ben

Franklins on the table. It also seemed like he wanted to win back, all in one hand, a lot of the 5K we heard he gambled away. Dad was dealing Jacks or better, but no one was opening, so with each new deal, everyone had to ante up $10 again. The pot was getting big, pretty fast, and no one had even opened or started bumping. After the fifth deal, it looked like at least 200 bucks in the pot, and then, after everyone else passed again, Lefty stood up, threw a $20 bill on the table, and said. "It's all gonna be my friggin' money, so I'll open for $20."

We all knew he had to have at least Jacks, and Lefty did not quite put on his poker face when he slammed the $20 on the table and howled, "If I lose this hand, I'll eat these friggin' cards!" Charlie and I were laughing while Lefty, putting on his goofy grin, pretended to nibble at his cards repeating over and over, "I'll eat these frigging cards." Peppy and Gino, even with $50 in the pot folded, only Uncle Piggy, Mr. Bones, and Tootsy matched the $20 opener.

Lefty threw down 2 cards singing to himself, "I'll eat these frigging cards. I'll eat these frigging cards," while betting another $10. "Holy shit!" Charlie almost knocked me over then elbowed me in the gut. "Sam, I bet he's got 3 Aces!" "At least 3 Jacks," I thought. Tootsy tossed in the $10 and drew 3 cards as did Mr. Bones. Now it was up to Uncle Piggy. I grabbed Charlie around the throat, squeezed him until he turned red when Piggy looked at Lefty, threw down two cards, and said calmly, "I'll see your $10 and bump you $20." Tootsy was a pretty good businessman, he ran the Senate Boys Pool Room and his own town numbers game, and he saw where this was going and decided to cut his losses right there, by throwing his arms to the ceiling and folding. Bones folded as well, ripping his losing hand and tossing the cards at Lefty, and in his pip-squeaky voice told Lefty, "Here you can eat these as well." Things got quiet as Dad dealt Lefty and Piggy two cards each. I watched as whatever poker face Lefty still had on left and turned into a big grin when he picked up his draw.

"I'll see your $20 and bump you $20," Lefty said and sat back while Piggy looked stone-faced at his own hand. "I'm in, and I call your hand," was all Piggy said as he calmly tossed two Andrew Jacksons on the table that was now a six-inch mound of Abes Bens and Georges.

"Full boat queens over sixes," Lefty whispered, threw his cards on the table, and started grabbing the dough, shoving the cash into his pockets while turning, looking for the quickest exit to 4th Street. "Hold everything, Lefty!" Dad yelled, loudly. "Can Piggy show his cards before you claim the pot and start pissing it away?" Everyone turned as Piggy, with the same stone-faced grin on his face, turned over his hand one card at a time, king of hearts, king of spades, king of clubs, eight of spades, eight of clubs, another full boat, and a bigger boat. Lefty tossed the cash back onto the table and stood motionless before all hell broke loose.

Big Mike, Mr. Bones, and Peppy grabbed Lefty and wrestled him to the ground, but even if his cancer-ridden body wasn't so weakened, the look on his face told me he had no fight left in him. "Eat these friggin' cards!" Peppy repeated over and over. "Eat these friggin' cards!" as Piggy tore his queens and sixes into little pieces and shoved them in Lefty's mouth while Gino grabbed his jaw and moved it up and down grinding his choppers helping Lefty keep his word. I knew Lefty had no will to fight back when he looked at me and Charlie and closed his eyes. I'm not sure I saw tears, but maybe my Dad and Big Mike did as they stepped in and pushed Peppy, Mr. Bones, and Uncle Piggy away.

"OK, guys, let him up. That's enough, it's not funny anymore," Big Mike said, holding back his own tears as he grabbed Gino, pulled his hands from Lefty's jaw and pushed him away just as Lefty struggled to stand up. I looked at Lefty, and now his tears were really flowing when Lefty looked first at me and then at Big Mike. I think Lefty was thinking the same thing as I was, that maybe Big Mike's not the total jerk we all thought he was? I'm pretty sure he will still treat my friends and me the same, but I think I'll look at him a little differently after tonight.

"Come on, you two," Dad said as he put his arms around me and Charlie, "I should have sent you kids home an hour ago." "It's OK, Mr. Moe, I mean Mr. Pagano." Charlie laughed, "We had a really great night." Dad walked us to the front door of The Arrow, gave me a fatherly kick in the butt, and told us to go the hell home.

While we never stopped going to the Arrow almost every day (until it became the Ure Inn), there was a lot less betting going on at the bar and many more card games going on in the backroom after my Dad was arrested one Saturday in November. I never understood why my Dad could not take bets from the guys while they all watched the horse races at Belmont, Aqueduct, or Yonkers, yet it was OK to hop into the back room and deal the cards and take two or three bets on every hand that was dealt out. All my friends told me that their dads were just as pissed as my Dad was and that he never forced anyone to make a bet and would tell Lefty or Mr. Bones or any of the guys to stop betting when they were on a losing streak. The Arrow was still the Arrow, and my Dad will always be one of the bookies in town, but after he was busted, most of the betting at The Arrow took place in the backroom in a card game not at the bar watching the ponies and eating the pizzas.

But things did not change at the local bars until November so on this Friday night after Lefty coughed up the card's and Dad kicked us out, we were left standing, pockets full of bucks outside The Arrow on the corner of 4th Street and Sherman Ave. The same corner where the first thing in the morning, the 39 bus would be dropping off and picking up lots of kids, moms, and dads going to Newark for fun, shopping, and work. It was almost 9 o'clock, too late for most kids to be out except for the Harrison or Kearny High School guys, and we really did not want to run into any of them. It would also be too late for The Twilight Zone and too early for the Midnight Movie even if my 13-inch black and white T.V. was fixed.

Outside The Arrow at the bus stop, even with the stars shining, it was pretty dark and sort of creepy. I stood there looking at Charlie and over my shoulder towards my house, thinking about the nutty night. Suddenly, I felt a sudden chill and really wanted to go home. From the bus stop, I could see around the corner onto 3rd Street, and although separated by two backyards, I saw the attic window and the second-floor attic roof of my house. From where I stood it was just a stone's throw from the bus stop at the Arrow to my attic window. I had never really seen my attic porch and window from that angle before, even though I sure spent a lot of time climbing on my roof and the roofs of half the houses in East Newark. Seeing just what a straight shot it was, I started thinking of some fun ideas. I could see how easy it would be to toss some eggs off of my roof right to this corner bus stop where I stood, no trees, a straight shot, and you would not need an arm like Kevin Gilmore to make the toss. I even thought about taking a few practice tosses when I got home.

Watching Charlie still pretending to slam his head into just about every parking meter as he headed home down 4th Street, I yelled out, "Call me tomorrow, Charlie."

"No can do. I'm going down the shore with Dominic and Angel," he yelled back.

"OK, I'll see ya on Monday," I mumbled and waved goodbye to Charlie and started my walk down Sherman Ave headed back home. Fifty feet into my journey I waived at Tony and Pete B. sitting on their front porch with Mr. and Mrs. Borghesi, Pete's house had this tremendous big screened-in front porch, and sometimes in the summer, friends, and neighbors would sit there and talk all night long. Pete waved back, ran off the porch, and I told him all about Lefty and the fun card game he missed. After we talked about some other things we could do on Saturday (I even told him about the view from the Arrow to my attic porch), and before he headed back to his parents' porch, I asked out loud, "What time you coming over tomorrow morning?"

I reminded Pete that last week (before our last-minute change of plans), we all pretty much agreed and were all set on going to this week's Saturday matinee. Along with a bunch of St. Anthony's, Harrison, and East Newark kids, we had all planned on meeting around 11:30 at the Warner Theater on 4th Street in Harrison.

All the kids in school were talking about the new Saturday matinee (something I have been talking about for weeks and weeks) called *Ghidorah, the Three-Headed Monster* featuring Godzilla, Rodan, and Mothra. I sure do want to see it, but I guess we could go next Saturday because Pete and I now agreed that this Saturday tossing some eggs off of my attic roof might be even more fun than a three-headed monster.

CHAPTER 9

The Saturday Matinee

"Are you kidding me, you don't want to go to see The Seventh Voyage of Sinbad?"

"It's gonna be a great movie," I assured Billy. "Well, wasn't I right about the *Angry Red Planet Rodan* and *Gorgo*?" "Yeah, Sammy, but what about *The Invasion of The Neptune Man?*" After seeing *The Invasion of The Neptune Man*, Billy had kind of lost faith in me. Somehow, I had convinced him and the Kyzinisky brothers last week that the Saturday movie about The Neptune Man would be as good or even better than *Rodan and Gorgo*.

"Yeah, just like *Varan The Unbelievable*? You also told us that piece of crap was going to be as good as Rodan and Gorgo," Teddy K said, grinning from ear to ear.

I had to give it to Teddy, *Varan The Unbelievable* was another monster movie I told everyone would be fun. Yet even I had to agree that until last week Varan was the worst movie we had ever seen. However, now that honor belongs to both *Varan The Unbelievable and The Invasion of The Neptune Men*. After agreeing that I had recommended some shitty movies lately, we also agreed to go see Sinbad at today's Saturday Matinee.

Me and Billy, Teddy and Eddie were walking down 4th Street in Harrison headed to the Warner Theater, when we passed the basketball courts and met up with Bobby Konsig (Bobby The K) and Charlie Lombardi. About halfway to the Warner, we all stopped at the sweet shop to fill up on penny candies and ran into Frankie Bachanes at the counter. Frankie wondered aloud, "Yeah, who the hell is going to pay five cents for a candy bar at the movies when you can get two for a nickel here?" And we all agreed that only the rich Kearny kids would. Frankie then leaned over the counter to grab a bag of *Milk Duds*, and at the same time, I noticed (as I usually did) that he slipped more than a few loose jellybeans into his pockets. Even though Frankie always complained that his dad never gave him any money, his pockets or sneakers were usually full of candy and sometimes full of coins.

Frankie was famous for finding every penny, nickel, or dime that anybody dropped on the sidewalk and for sticking his fingers into, the coin return slots of every payphone, candy, soda, and change machine in town. Always looking for and often finding even more quarters dimes and nickels.

"You coming to the Warner with us?" I asked Frankie. And when I saw the frown on his face, and he presented to me his empty sneaks and pockets (except for Jellybeans), I volunteered to buy his ticket. "OK, great! But what about Charlie and Stevie?" Frankie asked, about his brothers, grinning at me as he always did when he was trying to pick your pocket. "Come on, Frankie, I only have a buck! Your brothers are on their own."

Even though I had almost $1.50, there was no way I was buying a ticket for Charlie, who was about 15 and had a job at the sweet shop and especially not for Stevie, his younger little smarty pants of a brother.

By the time we got to the Warner theater, the line of kids was halfway around the block, and it was not even 11:30. "Jesus, maybe you got it right this time," Billy's jaw dropped as we began to count the number of kids in line. For months I had read about The Seventh Voyage of Sinbad in Monster magazine. And for the last few weeks, everyone who went to the Warner saw the previews for "Sinbad" featuring the One-Eyed Cyclops, and now here we were waiting in line with just about every other kid in town!

"Jump in," John Hess said as he pointed to the spot right behind him and right in front of Andrea Latini's dad. We didn't wait to hear her dad say, "Go ahead, guys." We jumped in just as he spoke and before he pointed to the spot in front of his two goofy six-year-old sons. Now, after our sneak in, we were only about 100 kids from the ticket window. Usually, it was a little harder to sneak in line, but Anthony Boehner, the regular Saturday matinee usher, was nowhere to be found. Anthony A.K.A. The Boner was missing in action.

Waiting in line, I told Frankie that even if I wanted to, I couldn't buy Charlie and Stevie's tickets. "Yeah, don't worry about it, just get me in, and I'll get them in when the lights go out." I had no idea what his plan to sneak them in was, but I figured it would be fun, especially since Frankie thought it up and a little tougher if the Boner finally showed up.

Anthony Boehner was about 18 years old and really kooky, or a little slow, as our parents would say. He was also tons of fun and our favorite usher. We called him Big Boner, and the Saturday matinee was just not the same when he wasn't there. I didn't want to get my hopes up too high, but then I heard some mom mention his name, so I guessed Anthony was somewhere on the job.

Finally, after 30 minutes in line (it seemed like two hours), we got our tickets and now got to wait in the popcorn line for another 15 minutes. Billy was really in a hurry to head upstairs and light up his loosie, so he begged Frankie.

"Please go get us some first-row seats in the balcony."

"Time out, Billy," Frankie interrupted. "You can have your smokes after we sneak in Charlie and Stevie" Billy wanted to sit in the balcony so he could smoke the loosies he got at Mollie's corner store, but this week he would have to wait till Frankie snuck in his brothers.

It looked like the first few front rows were all filled up, the lights were out, and the previews were about to start. Frankie then started looking for Big Boner, so he could borrow/grab his flashlight and help find us some seats next to the fire escape.

"Why the heck do you want to sit next to the fire escape?" I asked Frankie

"You will find out in five minutes," he cracked. I thought ah ha this must be part of the sneak in plan, so I helped Frankie find Boner, and we asked for his help. Whenever The Warner was running a double feature, you needed your ticket stub so you could go outside between shows, and then when the next show started, show your stub and get back in, so I thought I'll try the same trick I last used a few weeks ago.

"Anthony, I dropped my ticket. Can I borrow your flashlight, please?" I was guessing he wouldn't remember that I asked the same question many other times, I guessed right because he gave me the flashlight and just like last time, I started running full speed down the aisles yelling.

"Boner, where's my ticket? I lost my ticket!" It was dark now, so as I ran up and down the aisles, I pointed the flashlight to the floor, ceiling, screen, and to the balcony. Boner was actually running behind me, trying to help me find the ticket that I still had in my pocket, asking, "Where did you drop the ticket? What row were you near?"

"Row five, I think," I told him as I handed the flashlight off to Frankie, who turned around and ran toward the screen.

"We were down by row three Boner," Frankie was yelling, and half the kids in the Warner were yelling out where the ticket might be when the lights came back on, and the manager climbed up on the movie stage and told everyone the previews would not start until everyone stopped yelling and sat down. And for us that meant sitting down in the seats Anthony got us right next to the fire escape.

Things quieted down a bit after the manager, Boner, and some dads got everyone seated. I watched as Mr. Warner went up to the balcony and into the projection room, and within a minute, the screen came alive with the blurry testing 1, 2, 3, 4 as Mr. Warner was again trying to focus the camera on the screen.

"OK, I'm letting Charlie and Stevie in," Frankie whispered as he started crawling toward the fire escape and pushed the door open.

"Is he freaking nuts?" Billy asked me. Like I knew what he had planned. Hell, I don't think even Frankie had a clue about what was about to happen.

First, the intense daylight shined into the theater, and everyone turned to look at the suddenly open fire escape door. Then the sirens started blaring loudly, just as every other exit sign over every other door started flashing, the house lights came back on, and about 15 kids pushed through the open fire escape door and ran in 15 different directions.

It took a little longer for the manager to calm things down this time, even with the help of the fire chief, Mr. Howard, who was seated in the front row with his kids. The Harrison firemen got there in less than 10 minutes, and the alarms started blaring again when they pushed through the other fire escape door.

"What set off the alarm boss?" I heard one of the firemen say to Mr. Howard.

"I did, you know, just making sure you guys were on duty and not goofing off." Mr. Howard seemed to be calm, and in a funny mood now that he knew there was no fire.

"I thought just Charlie and Stevie would come in. I didn't know they would tell their friends!" Frankie was laughing, grinning ear to ear "And their friends would tell their friends, and every other frigging light in the place would go on, and every alarm would go off."

"Well, Frankie, I think everyone's on to your plan now." Billy laughed out loud. I was hoping that the lights would go out, the fire doors would close, and the cartoons and previews would finally start. Apparently, so was everyone else, as a big cheer went up when the lights went out and the testing 1,2,3,4 screen came back on. Now that we did not have to sit next to the fire escape and the funny Mickey Mouse and Farmer

Gray cartoons were sadly over, we finally moved up to the balcony so Billy could smoke his loosie.

I liked sitting in the balcony for lots of reasons, the number one reason was we were not allowed up there without our parents. However, that never stopped us from sneaking up to the top rows. We could sit right under the projector and toss popcorn into the light path firing out of the camera and poof just like that, tiny trails of darkness were flying across the screen in and out of the scene. It didn't matter if it was an army battle or a love scene, because suddenly out of nowhere, you would hear

"Look, mom! Up in the sky it's a bird it's a plane it's a meteorite flying through the air."

One Saturday last winter, seated in the balcony watching Rodan fly over and destroy Tokyo, Charlie and I started tossing my jacket up and down through the projector's light path, and Goddam it if didn't really look like the shadow of a giant bird (as big as Rodan) flying across the screen. A few times, we timed our toss perfectly with Rodan's flight, and the shadow on the screen was so real we heard someone say, "Holy shit now there are two Rodan's."

Another reason I liked the balcony was that all the teenage girls sat up there screaming their heads off watching Godzilla or necking with their boy-friends during the love scenes. Whatever they were doing, relaxing, necking, eating popcorn, they are always a lot of fun to watch.

The previews this Saturday were fun. I thought at least 2 of the 3 movies coming out soon would be a blast to see, but number one on everyone's list without a doubt would be *King Kong Vs. Godzilla* No one will miss that war, a war of the two most enormous monsters ever. In a few weeks, when King Kong and Godzilla finally square up, Tokyo despite surviving WW11 and Atom bombs was definitely a goner! *The Three Hundred Spartans and The Tingler* looked good, too. I remember once for homework last year having to, but not reading about the Spartans for History class. (I'm sure gonna read about them tonight) I hope they play The Spartans and King Kong and Godzilla together for a double feature of historic hero warriors and famous earth-shattering monsters.

Now that things finally calmed down, I was waiting for the show to begin, sitting way up in row two with Teddy and Eddie. Frankie and Billy were sitting right in front of us, in row one, at the edge of the balcony. Of course, that is the best row in the house for playing *bombs away*, and if Frankie wasn't such a cheapskate, I think he would have tossed down his whole bag of popcorn. So, every time he chucked a few at some kids down below, I reminded him that I bought him the popcorn, so at least he should let me get in a few tosses.

"When the hell is the movie going to start?" Eddie wondered out loud excitedly, which was precisely what everyone was else was wondering. Eddie was getting a little antsy as were most of the parents, why else would half the Dads be pleading with Boner pointing at the screen and looking at their watches?

Once again, the lights went out, and this time the credits started to roll for *The Seventh Voyage of Sinbad*. I had waited too long and was not going to let everyone forget who dragged them to see this movie. So I stood up, on the top of my balcony seat one inch from the railing and proclaimed. "Ladies and gentlemen, I present to you the greatest, most fantastic movie in the history of the Warner Theater, Da Da Da Dah "The Seventh Voyage" of Eh Duh? Oh yeah, Sinbad!"

I knew Teddy (and everyone else) was getting tired of listening to me go on and on about Sinbad for the last five years, but finally, now I knew I could watch him sit back, put his popcorn down and see his jaw drop, as the screen came alive. For the next hour and a half, no one left their seat, not even to hit the head, smoke a loosie buy some *Milk Duds*, or even to sneak up to the balcony to toss some popcorn.

We watched as Sinbad and his crew got lost at sea and accidentally landed on the island of Colossal. That's where they first meet Sokurah, the evil magician, as he is fleeing from a giant one-eyed Cyclops. Sokurah somehow gets away from the Cyclops by ordering the Genie, from his magic lamp, to create an invisible wall. But, when the Cyclops tossed a giant boulder breaking the wall, the Cyclops grabbed the magic lantern and started to rub it.

"This can't be good," I thought.

Over the next hour and a half, we watch Sinbad leave Colossal, a slave girl turn into an eight-armed snake woman, an army of sword-fighting skeletons battle a giant two-headed Roc, (another Cyclops). Then after a fire-breathing Dragon in a secret cave battles Sinbad Sokurah secretly shrinks the princess Parisa to Six inches tall.

After Sokurah tells Sinbad the only way to get his princess back to size is to recover the magic lamp from the Cyclops, Sinbad has no choice but to return to Colossal.

Once Sinbad gets back to Colossa, we meet the sword fighting skeletons who, for some reason, have pirate patches where they do not have eyes. Sinbad keeps stabbing them between the bones, so killing the dead skeletons is almost impossible. Finally, Sinbad figures out to swing his sword like a baseball bat and just smash them to bits. All this happens just in time to encounter the two-headed Roc, whose eggs are crucial to restoring Princess Parisa to full size.

We sat as quiet as the Genie, whose only spoken words the whole movie were, "I shall try master, I shall Try!" helps Sinbad escape from the two-headed Roc, and beheads the Cyclops. The Genie holding the Cyclops head then stabs the Dragon, who falls on and kills Soku-rah. Finally the Genie restores Parisa Sinbad's princess to full height.

For his reward, he is granted his wish to become a real 12-year-old boy and Sinbad's, first mate. The final scene has the Genie now a real boy stand-ing on the deck, mast in hand sailing into the unknown that will become

The 8th Voyage of Sinbad. When they arrive, I'll be there, and I know the Warner theater will be packed.

But, unless Sinbad embarks on his Eighth Voyage by next week, Billy and I agreed that we would be sitting in the same seats watching the Seventh Voyage once again.

Still shaking in my pants I got up from my seat slowly, hoping, somehow, that Boner would start the previews all over again. Everyone seemed to feel the same as they all began to scratch their heads as they headed for the aisles while watching the credits roll. Everyone seemingly searching for an answer as to how the hell they made those monsters come to life. On the way down from the balcony, we finally ran into Bobby and Charlie. Literally, we ran into them, as everyone was starting to get a little crazy rushing into the long line to get to the stairway. That's when Bobby started practicing his football skills. Even though Bobby the K. goes to Lincoln School, way on the other side of Harrison, we have a mutual friend in Charlie, so we also became buddies. Charlie used to go to Lincoln with Bobby, but because of all the fights and D's on his report card, his parents sent him to St. Anthony's. So now Charlie gets into fights at St. A's, the three of us are friends, and Charlie still gets D's.

We were walking shoulder to shoulder down from the balcony with the other two hundred kids when suddenly everything came to a halt when we merged with the three hundred kids and parents on the main floor. We were just about 50 feet from the two swinging exit doors when everyone came to a dead stop.

"Oh my God, I tripped," Bobby laughed out loud, as he kneeled in front of Charlie. "Trip on this!" Charlie answered as he pushed Billy on top of Bobby.

"Pile On!" I yelled, pushing Eddie, Teddy and Charlie on, before jumping on top myself. It did not take very long before there were three piles of fifteen or twenty kids, each pile getting bigger by the second. The pile ons were always fun unless you got stuck on the bottom, and this time I sure did!

"Get the hell off of me!" I screamed. I was stuck under Stevie K. and 15 other kids. I couldn't move an inch and didn't think this was funny anymore. I kind of figured I was stuck under Stevie because his short leg with the wooden peg and six-inch boot was sticking right in my face. Somehow, I was able to crawl out from under the pile. And with the help of Boner, the manager, and a few parents, we were able to keep even more kids from jumping on. The parents and the manager finally stopped any new pile ons and started to pull everyone off. Every time the manager would bend over to pull someone off, Bobby would pretend to help him while coughing up a big gob on his back. "I'll help you, Mr. Warner, I'll help you," cough, cough, gob, gob.

"Holy Shit did you see his back?" Bobby was laughing so hard I really thought he would choke to death.

"I can't believe you actually gobbed on his uniform" Teddy must have said that to Bobby 25 times, as we headed back up fourth street. Teddy obviously had a new hero. It was only around four in the afternoon, so we all stopped at the sweet shop again to buy some fries and a root beer. Well, except for Frankie, who again swore he was dead broke. The sweet shop was filling up with the high school kids, so we had to stand at the counter and shoot spitballs through a straw to get Ronnie Cat's attention. Everyone else who worked at the sweet shop would not even bother to give us a look, forget about taking our order.

"Look, there's Mary Ann!" I whispered. Frankie knew I liked her and was afraid to talk to her, but when her girlfriend, Andrea, who lived way down on Second Street, got up and walked away,

I walked over to the table and almost shouted.

"Mary Ann, did you see Sinbad at the matinée?"

"Ssshhh! Yes, and I saw you guys diving all over each other in the lobby. That was really stupid."

"Yeah, I really got stuck at the bottom of a pile," I told her and agreed it was stupid and dangerous, but it was Bobby's idea. "Yeah you had nothing to do with it, are you kidding me. I saw you push Teddy and Eddie to help-start the crazy mess."

"Oh, you saw that, well, Bobby dared me, so I had no choice. You understand that, don't you?" I said, trying to change the subject.

I asked Mary Ann if she saw the previews for *The Three Hundred Spartans or The Tingler*, and started to ask if she would go see them with me, but I knew I wanted to see it with the guys, so I asked if she wished to have some fries instead. "No, thanks," she smiled and left to find Andrea. I just stood there with a sleepy frown on my face until

Teddy snuck up behind and gave me a kick in the ass. That really woke me up.

At least I had the nerve to ask Mary Ann about the movie. Last week I walked her home from school, and when we got to her house, I just stood there silently, twiddling my thumbs for about six hours. We keep looking at each other's eyes, and every few minutes, I tried to say something, anything when finally Mary Ann picked up her book bag mumbled, "See ya in class tomorrow," walked up the steps to her house at 33 Davis Ave and slammed the door behind her.

It will be at least 2-3 weeks before The Tingler comes to the Warner cause Sinbad (along with every kid in town) will definitely be back next Saturday. After seeing Sinbad, today and I hope the next three Saturday's we should know just about every line by heart. I know that I might not know every line by next week but "I shall try master I shall try."

That's next week but this week, everyone was still sitting on the edge of their seats with eyes glued to the screen when the dying Cyclops fell and crushed Sokurah again. I decided that it would be a really great time to break out the surprise gift I got on the Wildwood boardwalk this summer. As everyone stood up to clap and cheer for the Genie just as he becomes a 12-year-old boy, I threw my arms overhead and released the stink perfume. I kept the Stink Perfume locked away in my mom's jewelry box for months, waiting for such a perfect moment, and this was the perfect moment. I knew it smelled like rotten eggs, but I had only tried it outside in my back yard. Never inside a house or a movie theater with 500 people inside! Well, that became about 20 people after about ten minutes of that beautiful rotten egg aroma. The smell was so bad and spread so quickly, I thought the stink perfume must have gone bad, became rotten, expired, or something? Nothing could smell that shitty!

"Where the hell did you get that crap? Bobby begged. Do you have more? You have to give me some!" Bobby was having a canary, as we stood outside the Warner, waiting for the smell to die down and the Warner to reopen. Frankie and Bobby knew it was me who tossed the fart perfume. Still, I was terrified of anyone else finding out, especially the family right behind us who got soaked in it. Usually, the stuff I bought at the gift shop on the boardwalk was fun, like bomb bags or X-ray glasses. But nothing would ever live up to its ad like the stink perfume did. Why the hell didn't I get 10 bottles?

Now it's August and Sinbad's record run at the Warner was over, and everyone was talking about the end of summer and looking forward to going back to school. I was looking forward to finally seeing the Tingler, but Mary Ann and all the girls wanted to see some movie about The Beatles? Whoever the hell they are! I finally got the nerve to ask Mary Ann to go see the Tingler with me on Tuesday at five o'clock, but not to the Saturday matinee. I still wanted to go to the Matinee with Charlie.

Mary Ann had red hair, freckles, and a cute dopey smile. But to me, she was a pretty, cute, happy smirky cartoon gal.

A lot less scary to yours truly than some other 6th grade girls like Janet, Andrea, or Debbie. Whenever I thought about Janis, Andrea or Debbie St. John, I got all nervous, when I thought about Mary Ann, I just laughed. I especially loved the way she would raise her eyebrows and curl up her nose and lips when I said something stupid, which was fairly often.

The Tingler is about this tiny centipede creature that lies dormant in everyone's spine. When people get terrified of anything, The Tingler comes alive, starts to grow bigger and bigger, curling around crushing and eating your spine. The only thing that can and always stops your Tingler is when you panic, scream, or cry out loud.

During the previews, the director of the movie talked about something called

Percepto. He told us how we (the audience) would feel the same sensation and experience the same shock as the victims in the movie, but he explained to the audience how to protect ourselves (yell, cry, scream) from the Tingler.

The last time I saw a movie (Scent of Mystery) that promised something like Percepto, it was smell-o-vision (ah smell those dead skunks), and although smell-o-vision worked pretty good and was a hit, my stink perfume at the end of Sinbad was way more effective.

On Tuesday's or almost any weekday night at the Warner, there were fewer kids, a lot more teenagers, and depending on the feature, even some adults without kids. For *The Tingler*, we got terrific seats in the third row right on the aisle. We hoped *The Tingler* was as scary as the previews promised, but still, we had no idea what Percepto was. We soon found out. In the movie, a centipede, AKA, the Tingler was crawling up some deaf and dumb lady's spine, and when she tried to scream, nothing came out, so about 25 of the people in the Warner cried out-loud for her, including Mary Ann.

Why?

The Tingler had crawled up their spines.

Percepto was a real hit. Someone who worked at the Warner, I doubt it was Boner, installed buzzers in the back of some of the seats. So, every time *The Tingler* was crawling up, and about to crush a deaf and dumb victim's spine, the seat buzzers would go off against their spine, and the moviegoers would supply the screaming.

When the buzzers went off the first time, I saw lots of people jump up and scream. The second time they went off Mary Ann jumped right into my arms, and for the rest of the movie, I squeezed and held her hand.

So, while Vincent Price experimented with LSD to scare some of his patients so they would scream and stop *The Tingler* from creeping up their spines, I thought about kissing Mary Ann to stop her from shrieking. And to stop watching the Tingler so intensely and somehow pay more attention to me.

The next time the buzzers went off, she grabbed my hand and almost jumped in my lap. I gave her a little peck on the cheek, and then when she did not slap me but squeezed my hand even harder, I took a deep breath and put my lips right against hers. I touched her lips with my lips, and my tongue touched her tongue and then almost choked on a big wad of popcorn in my mouth. Mary Ann burst out laughing, saying even louder, "You did tell me you wanted some popcorn."

"That was even better than *The House on Haunted Hill*," I said as The Tingler came to an end.

Mary Ann shook her head. "Never saw that one," she also asked if it had buzzers in the seats.

"Na, that one had a giant skeleton that flew over our heads right in the middle of the scary parts."

As we walked back up Fourth Street, on the way home, we ran into Bobby and Charlie. I told them about *The Tingler* and how we were all in for a treat on Saturday. As soon as I mentioned going on Saturday with the guys, I bit my tongue, thought about asking Mary Ann again, but figured I really should go see "The Tingler" with the guys.

When we got to Mary Ann's house on North Second Street, it was starting to get dark. I tried to put my hand in hers when she pushed me away, laughing, "You must want some more popcorn?"

Walking away from her house, I asked, "So, will I See you tomorrow at the sweet shop after school?"

"I don't know, maybe, maybe not," Mary Ann smiled and ran up her porch steps.

OK, more popcorn with Mary Ann or fun with the guys, mushy popcorn or stink perfume? I wanted both, but since I already told Bobby about the Tingler, I figured Mary Ann and I could go see the new dopey Beatles? Or the Cockroaches? Whoever that new band was in a few weeks.

Watching "The Tingler" on Saturday was almost as much fun as it was with Mary Ann. Especially, because both Bobby and Charlie got seats with the buzzers. I really thought they would want to kill me the first time they went off, and I almost laughed to death.

"You knew they were in our seats?" Bobby asked.

"Yeah, well, I didn't know, but I sure was hoping they were," I confessed. It turned out after the first shock, Bobby and Charlie both couldn't wait for

the buzzers to go off and kept switch-
ing seats to see who had the best buzzer. Bobby even tried to rip open his
seat and rip the buzzer out, but Boner
caught him in the act.

I sure planned on asking Mary Ann to go
see the Beatles (we now called them the
Roaches) with me. But before the Beatles
hit the big screen, I did enjoy a few more
monster movies with the guys, then spent
a few great weeks down the shore with
my family and didn't even mind missing
two Saturday Matinees at the Warner.
But even though I thought about it before we left and when I got back from the
shore, I just never got up the nerve to ask
Mary Ann to see the Beatles with me.

"A Hard Day's Night" was the Beatles
movie that we heard about every day.
We saw the previews, saw them on Ed

Sullivan, and now we even listened to the songs on the radio, especially on WABC. Cousin Brucie could not stop talking about the Beatles or calling himself the fifth Beatle.

"Are we really going to see those hippies?" Bobby did not like the Beatles and really did not like it when the girls said they were better than the Four Seasons or even better than Elvis.

Come on, Bobby, "I like, *Can't Buy me Love,* that's a pretty good song." I said it just to get Bobby pissed, but I really did like it and still do.

Bobby started dancing, grabbed my hand, and said, "Yeah, Sammy, it's a real toe-tapper."

I really did want to go see the Beatles on Saturday. I mean, after a few weeks down the shore, I would have gone back to the Matinee even if *Invasion of the Neptune Men* was playing again.

The plan was for me and Pete to meet at his house and head straight to the sweet shop. That's where we would meet Charlie and Bobby and the rest of the crew and head on over to the Warner after filling up on penny candies.

We were across from the Two Guys Store when I saw the line. "Oh my God, it's all girls." It wasn't really, but it sure looked like it was five to one, five girls to every guy.

"Come on, Pete," I said, all excited because I saw Mary Ann right next to Teddy and Eddie in the middle of the line, and we jumped in, right in front of my cousins Vinnie and Debbie .

"Sam, do you see Boner? If he saw us jump in, we are going to get in trouble." Pete was a little timid about sneaking in line, and when Uncle Vinnie flashed his chief of police badge, he almost crapped in his pants.

"It's OK, Pete, you just have to be careful when you listen to my nephew little, Sammy."

"OK, Uncle Vinnie, I'll never do it again," Pete said, a little shaken up.

"Listen to little Moe, I mean," Uncle Vinnie said, smiling at me.

The line moved pretty fast, and pretty soon we were somehow sitting in the front row watching previews of "Children of the Dammed." It looked terrifying, the children looked like their eyes would explode right out of their heads, kind of like Billy's eyes sometimes looked.

Because of the size of the ticket lines and how everyone was talking about the Beatles, we knew we would have to wait a few weeks for *The Children of the Dammed*, but as Ed Sullivan said.

"Right here right now, on our stage, ladies and gentlemen The Beatles!" As soon as the cartoons and previews were over, the title and credits were running across the screen. At the same time, the Beatles were running away from every teenage girl in London. As the song "A Hard Day's Night" played, we got to see the long-haired freaks up close from the first row. Every girl in the Warner was screaming, "Paul, John, George, Ringo." The movie was silly. While The

Beatles are getting ready for a show, Ringo gets lost in London, and the rest of The Beatles are running around trying to find him in time for the show.

Bobby really thought the movie was stupid, and the Beatles were a bunch of stupid Hippies. "They dress like girls and sing like girls." I thought the movie was fun, and every five minutes, they played a song that drove the girls at The Warner nuts. In between songs, the boys try desperately to find Ringo, who is still running around London totally lost. Ringo even got falsely and comically arrested in one scene.

Since I was a little kid, I have seen my friends and the high school boys, do some crazy things at The Warner, but I never saw anyone except the Manager or Boner climb on the stage during a show. That is until today, every time the Beatles got together to practice, or a song played in the background, five, ten, even fifteen twelve to fourteen-year-old girls climbed onto the stage and started screaming at and hugging the screen. Mr. Warner also stopped the movie once, and Boner jumped on stage and asked everyone to stay in their seats.

In the movie John, Paul and George finally find Ringo in time for the giant stadium show in London. Pete and I were really enjoying the film, and when The Beatles broke out singing, "She Loves You, Yeah, Yeah, Yeah." The gals in the Warner went nuts. There must have been 20 girls, including Mary Ann, jumping on the stage screaming at the Beatles, trying to hug them, and kiss the screen. The screen started to shake so much that it looked like The Beatles *A Hard Day's Night* was a 3D movie.

Bobby did not think this was fun at all. He was screaming, "Get the hell off the stage." That's when he got really pissed and climbed up on stage himself and started grabbing the gals one by one and pushing them away from the screen still screaming, "Get off the stage." As I moved up to get as close to the stage as I could, Pete stood there frozen with the same look on his face as when Uncle Vinnie flashed his badge. As I got back to our front row seats right below the stage, I saw Boner climbing up on the other side of the stage again trying to calm things down, that's when Bobby grabbed Mary Ann and pushed her so hard she tripped and started falling off the stage.

I guess I was in the right spot at the right time, I caught her in my arms and stopped her from crashing right on the floor. I heard a bunch of adults yelling at Bobby and Boner, shouting, "Get off the stage! Stop the movie."

Then I looked at Mary Ann, put my arms around her, puckered my lips, and she smiled at me, curled up her nose and lips, looked me right in the eyes, and said, "Boy, oh boy Sammy, you will do anything to get some popcorn won't you?"

CHAPTER 10

Where Were You 50 Years Ago

The day was July 20, 1969, a day our parents, teachers, and our President had been talking about forever. On this day, America was hoping to land a man

on the moon, and even more important-
ly, the New York Mets were in first place!

It was around three in the afternoon. I
could already smell the meatballs that
my Mom was cooking up for dinner,
A.K.A. "Sunday Pasta." I was 16, enjoying every moment of the summer,
and trying hard not to think about
September and my Senior year of high
school. Since the end of June, Sunday
afternoons had become the day when
Mary Ann, (My sweet 16 girlfriend)
and I would make our weekly ten-dol-
lar intercontinental phone call. This
Sunday, it was my turn to call Australia, tell Mary Ann how much I missed
her and update her on what was going
on in her old stomping grounds. East
Newark, all 12 blocks of it, and in Harrison, New Jersey.

Mary Ann and I had been going steady for almost four months - a long time for high school kids - when her Dad's company asked him to open a new branch in Australia. He ignored my advice (let Mary Ann stay here with her uncle), jumped at the opportunity, and took his family overseas. Mary Ann and I both agreed that being 10,550 miles away for a few months was not a big deal, would only make us miss each other, and we would continue to go steady. Once our parents got over the fact that N.J. Bell would charge around ten bucks for a three-minute overseas phone call, we decided that Sunday afternoon (lowest rates) would be the best time, and Mary Ann would make the first overseas call as soon as they landed in Australia.

I was hoping, on that Sunday, July 20, and asked again and again like I did every Sunday if her Dad had decided he didn't like his job after all, (or got fired) and his family would be boarding the next flight back to Newark.

"Is your Dad ready to come back to East Newark?"

"No, Sammy, he really likes going to work every day and is loving how he is starting to speak with an Australian accent."

"An Australian accent, what does he do talk like a kangaroo?"

"Very funny, no, kind of like a Platypus."

So, instead of a plane ride home, we talked about our friends, families, and the kangaroo that Mary Ann saw on a beach in Melbourne.

I also wanted to talk to Mary Ann about maybe going to a rock concert. (I thought my friend Kevin said a bunch of bands would be playing in the woods?) I didn't want my Mom to hear about it so, before asking, I stepped into the family bathroom down the hall from my sister Dianne's room. (Her rotary pink Princess phone had a 50-foot cord so I could go from room to room.) It was when I asked Mary Ann if she might be home in time to drive with our friend Kevin up to the concert in the woods, that I heard a laugh. She shot back, "Next month, are you nuts? We are not coming home next month, maybe not even next year!"

"Next Year, you're kidding, right?" "Please don't tell me that! I thought you said you would be back by the end of summer?"

"Sammy, we love it here, and my Dad wants to stay, and his work wants him to stay."

"But, you told me…"

"OK, Sammy, this whole thing is not working, so let's just stop pretending we are dating and just be friends."

That's when I cried out loud, "Mary Ann, you are breaking my heart. Please come home!"

The next thing I heard was my Mom banging on the bathroom door, "Sammy, come out here quick, you have to see this."

"What, Mom? What do you want? I don't want to see anything!"

"You need to come out here now. It's on T.V.! AMERICANS ARE WALKING ON THE MOON. NEIL ARMSTRONG IS THE FIRST MAN ON THE MOON!!!"

"Mom, I don't give a hoot who the heck is walking on the moon. Don't you get it? Mary Ann is breaking up with me! Oh my God, Mom, why on earth would I care about somebody stomping on the stupid moon?" I am getting dumped!

Well, it's almost 50 years later, and whenever I think about, hear or see the replay of the first Moon Walk, one of America's and mankind's greatest achievements, I smile. I smile because, over time, I came to understand how missing that historic event in real-time contributed to a memorable moment in my life.

Most of the 530 million people who watched it live can tell you exactly where they were on that day. While I didn't see the step or hear the quote, "That's one small step for man, one giant leap for mankind." I sure remember exactly where I was at that moment on that memorable day. In the bathroom on a pink rotary phone with my soon-to-be ex-girlfriend! Do you remember where you were?

For years after that day, I had a feeling that somehow the moon landing and Neil Armstrong had come between Mary Ann and me. I now understand it was the Atlantic Ocean and the real world, money and a job-that pushed us apart while Neil and the walk kinds of binds us together.

Oh, and Mary Ann came back to America a few years later, and we remain friends to this day. Only now because she moved again, we are so called social media friends but it still feels like the real thing to us.

It was almost a month after my heartbreak, and I was almost over that historic event in my teenage life when I started to hang out again with my high school and East Newark buddies. I also stopped listening to A.M. radio and my old favorites like The Four Seasons, Dion, and Bobby Darin. Along with all my friends, I started listening to F.M. radio hearing more of The Beatles, The Stones, The Who, and The Dead.

I was also hearing a little more about the concert in the woods Kevin Duffy told me about last month, the one I hoped Mary Ann would go to with Kevin and me. Apparently, some of these new F.M. rock groups might be playing at the concert, and it would only be an hour and a half drive from East Newark and Harrison.

So, while I was hearing about the concert, I was much more focused on the great baseball season watching the 5th place Yankees and the 2nd place Mets. But then, one day, while walking up Cleveland Ave. I ran into Kevin.

"Kev, you still thinking of going to that concert in the N.Y. woods?" I asked while I passed by his front porch on my way to Mike's Deli.

"I wasn't Sammy, but since Cindy left me for Ronnie and Mary Ann left you for a kangaroo, we might as well go take a shit in the woods."

"I think Its next week, right, Kev?"

"Not really sure, but they are talking about it a lot on WNEW, let me listen to what they are saying later, and if it sounds good, and I can borrow my dad's car for the day, I'll give you a call tomorrow."

For the first time in a month, I was looking forward to a call. I even asked my older sister Dianne (still a Four Seasons, Elvis, and Paul Anka gal) if she might be interested, knowing if Dianne was going, my Mom would definitely let me go.

"The Who? Who will be playing? No, actually, I hate those hippie bands, but I'll tell Mom it will be safe and fun, and she should let you go."

"OK, please talk to Mom for me tell her Kevin is a perfectly good driver."

Then she laughed and mumbled something about a fender bender he had and about that bunch of freaking hippies, also known as long hair freaky people who need to get a haircut and get a real job!

On Saturday, August 16, we were all set to go. Kev had his Dad's 64 Bonneville Coupe (gas tank filled), and between us, we also had an extra $40 for tickets to the concert, lunch, and gas if we ran out. We hit the road about 10:30 that morning and figured we would get to the show in the woods about 12:30 just in time for some lunch and rock & roll. With a Rand McNally map of New Jersey and New York and about twenty quarters for pay-phones just in case we had to call home, we started flying up Highway 287, looking for the exit to Highway 87. I kinda think Kevin hit

60 or even 65 M.P.H. a few times, and I think he would've kept pushing the pedal to the metal if his Dad's Bonneville did not sound like it was about to explode.

We were flying up Highway 87 when the map pointed us to highway NY 17, and we started to pass little towns with mom and pop stores, a few people some golf courses, and lots of cows. After riding on NY 17 for thirty miles, things started to slow down when we saw a giant lake, and according to the map, White Lake was only 5 miles from Bethel NY, the home base of the concert.

Traffic on 17 continued to slow down for about ten minutes, and then it stopped! We were stuck in a highway parking lot; cars were backed up fender-to-fender as far as our eyes could see.

"Oh my God, Kev, this is the perfect time to let me drive."

Since we were only going about half a mile an hour, Kevin agreed to let me sit behind the wheel until things picked up.

"OK, but over 5 M.P.H., and I am back behind the wheel," Kevin warned.

We were kind of on a slight downhill, so I never even had to put the stick shift into first gear. I just shifted from park to neutral and rolled ten to twenty feet every two to three minutes.

"What the hell is going on?"

Kevin was looking at the gas left in the tank, watching the Hippies park their cars on the side of the highway, getting out, and starting the long walk towards Bethel singing out of tune and full of joy. "On our way to Bethlehem."

With Kev back behind the wheel, we tried a few side roads that went no-where and were ten times slower. We also started to see cars on the grassy hills fifty feet off the road and the hip-pies putting up tents.

It was almost three in the afternoon when the word started to spread from car to car and even on the car radios, that it would take about three more hours before we got close enough to even think about buying tickets.

"Three more hours? OK, Sammy, this is total bullshit. What the freak is going on?"

"I know Kev, when did you tell your Dad you would have the car home? I swore to my Mom I'd back by nine."

Even if we got to the concert at five-thirty or six, we would have to leave before seven to get back before nine, nine-thirty, this ain't going to work.

"Even if the goddam Who is ready to rock, whoever the hell the Who are-we still have to roll!" I said. "The closer we get, the worse this is going to get."

"OK, Sammy, let's turn the ship around load up the 8-track player, listen to The Who on WNEW, and we'll hear the same songs they'll be playing in the woods," answered Kev.

"Sure, what the hell, but can I drive until we start going over 5 M.P.H.?" I asked.

"Sure, I might even take a nap while you are inching along," replied Kev while pretending to snore.

It took only about two hours of crawling on the grass and side roads till I started to see the speedometer move, then Kev woke up and took the wheel, and within five minutes, we were hitting 60 on 87 again. Not having to buy tickets, we had plenty of cash for gas, dinner, and ice cream at a truck stop just as we drove into Jersey.

Finally, we made it back to East Newark, just before curfew and after twelve hours on the road. We laughed about the fun road trip and agreed we didn't care at all about missing a few rock bands. "Who cares if we missed seeing The Who, "We had no idea if they would be playing, but we got a laugh out of saying it over and over again."

At times over the weeks, months, and years to follow, we regretted turning around one mile from Woodstock. Kev always said, "If I knew it was going to be such a historic event, maybe I could have called dad and asked if we could have stayed overnight?"

"First of all, how the hell could you call? I don't think we saw a single pay-phone until we got back on NY 17, and it didn't matter cause my Mom would never have let me stay!"

"Yeah but if my dad let me stay, then you could have hitchhiked home!"

"OK Thumbs up to that Kev"

So, while 500,000 people or more made it to Woodstock, we were among the few who turned around. Turned around about one mile from being part of making history. I still feel historic every time I hear Sweet Judy Blue Eyes sing the chorus (well the way I hear it) "By the time we almost got to Woodstock we were half a million strong." Well, a half a million minus at least T.W.O.!

Looking back on the summer of 1969, the Summer of Love, I often regret missing the moon landing and not even spending one day celebrating that summer of love at Woodstock even though I was barely a mile away. However, I do have one great memory of, by far, the most fabulous event of that unforgettable summer.

And it wasn't the Moon Landing, Woodstock, Stonewall Riots, The Beatles breakup, Jets winning the Super Bowl, Manson murders or our troops starting to come home from Vietnam.

Summer was over, and I learned a big lesson from all my near misses. I wish I had learned how to work harder on my personal shortcomings or my high school study habits. Instead, what I learned was how not to miss a single inning of any baseball game. In fact, I don't think I even missed a pitch as the New York Mets-The Miracle Mets-became world champions and took over the top spot in the life-changing historical events of 1969!

ABOUT THE AUTHOR

Mr. Pagano's stories have been published in the Daily Record, The Sunday Star Ledger, and in Reminisce Magazine. He retired from the tech industry after 30 years of climbing telephone poles and fixing everything from switchboards to computer networks. Since retiring from the tech world he has spent the last 20 years on another lifelong passion, working as a personal trainer at the Madison NJ YMCA. He specializes in training special needs clients.

Mr. Pagano has also coached or organized youth Baseball teams from T-Ball to college level programs for over 30 years and now volunteers as a friendly visitor, visiting WWII vets for lunch. He lives with his wife Pam in Morris Township NJ. Together they raised two children Peter and Tom, and two pups Cody and Ellie.

Made in the USA
Middletown, DE
15 August 2023